Thomas Hood: The Uncrowned Laureate

Portrait of Thomas Hood as a young man

Thomas Hood: The Uncrowned Laureate

Peter Thorogood

Edited by Alan Durden

Bramber Press

First published in 2024 by
Bramber Press
St. Mary's House
Bramber
West Sussex
BN44 3WE
Email: info@bramberpress.co.uk
www.bramberpress.co.uk

ISBN 978-1-905206-17-9

Design and formatting by Alan Durden

Publications by Peter Thorogood

A Sent-to-Coventry Carol and Other Verses, or, Men, Women, and Other Beasts. Autolycus Press (1961 OP)

Love, said the Astronomers, and Other Poems. Autolycus Press (1961 OP)

Translations and Elaborations from Federico Garcia Lorca. British Council Poets (1970 OP)

Thomas Hood and 'The Progress of Cant': *A Study in Iconography . Papers in Research and Criticism.* Ed. D.Hawes. Polytechnic of Central London (1977 OP)

'Thomas Hood: A Nineteenth Century Author and his Relations with the Book Trade to 1835.' In *Development of the English Book Trade, 1700-1899.* Ed. Robin Myers and Michael Harris. Oxford Polytechnic. (1981. 2nd impression 1982, 3rd impression 1983 OP)

Thomas Hood: Poems Comic and Serious. With an introduction and notes. Bramber Press (1995)

The Witty and the Tender Hood. Readings for performance, arranged by Peter Thorogood. Bramber Press (1999)

In These Places ...At These Times: Selected Poems 1950-1975, With watercolours and pen-and-ink sketches by the author. Bramber Press (1997)

St Mary's Bramber: A Sussex House and its Gardens. Bramber Press (1998).

St Mary's Bramber: A Pictorial Souvenir Illustrated. Bramber Press (1998).

The Complete Comic and Curious Verse of Peter Thorogood. Bramber Press (2006) Illustrated with comic pen-and-ink sketches by the author.

South of the River: A Novel of the Fifties. Bramber Press (2005)

Could I Hear That Again, Please?: Views and Reviews of a Well-tuned Listener Articles for the BBC weekly magazine *The Listener* 1966-67. Bramber Press (2006)

Phoenix of Drury Lane: The Sensational Story of London's Greatest Theatre, Bramber Press (2022)

Edited works

Late Flowerings: Poems for Aurelia. Diana Dykes. Edited with a foreword by Peter Thorogood. Bramber Press (2002)

The Tale of Septimus Jones and *The Tale of Sylvester Doo.* Garnet Durham. Illustrated. For young children. Illustrated by Charles Coleman. Edited by Peter Thorogood. Bramber Press (2005)

Portrait of Village Life: Beeding and Bramber with Botolphs in Sussex. Miniature essays by Sussex local historian Keith Nethercoate Bryant. Collated, edited and illustrated, with a biographical introduction and notes. Bramber Press (2011)

Two Hearts that Would be True. Poems by twin sisters Margaret and Brenda Carpenter. With biographical introductions by Peter Thorogood.

ABOUT THE AUTHOR

PETER THOROGOOD was educated at Brentwood School (1937-1945), after which he spent a gap year at the London School of Economics (1946-47), where his tutors were Harold Laski, Chairman of the Labour Party, and distinguished criminologist, Karl Mannheim. He proceeded to Trinity College, Dublin (1948-52), where he read Modern Languages (French and Italian), after which he was appointed Director of Studies at the British School of Milan, being promoted to Vice-Principal in 1957.

In 1960, he became Lecturer in English Studies at the British Council in London and, as a visiting lecturer, went on special academic assignments to Bulgaria and Poland under the Communist regimes. He lectured on summer schools in Germany, Greece and Israel, the latter during the Six-Day War. In 1969, he joined the Polytechnic of Central London (now part of the University of Westminster) as Senior Lecturer in English Language and Literature in charge of evening courses, and was subsequently elected a Member of the Academic Council in 1979.

Peter retired in 1984 to take on the task of rescuing the medieval pilgrim inn, St. Mary's, in Bramber, Sussex, in partnership with the conservator and designer, Roger Linton DesRCA. Together, with the help of teams of local volunteers for nearly 40 years, they succeeded in bringing the house and gardens back to the splendour it is today and to open it to the public during the spring and summer seasons. For ten years Peter was, concurrently, 'Key-Keeper' of Bramber Castle (National Trust) on behalf of English Heritage management. Peter and Roger both received MBEs for conservation and the arts in the Queen's 80th Birthday Honours in 2006.

Peter Thorogood is a Fellow of the Society of Antiquaries and over sixty years a Fellow of the Royal Society of Arts. He is a leading authority on the life and work of the Victorian poet, Thomas Hood, and has, over the years, brought together one of the finest collections in private hands of first editions of Hood's works, as well as autograph letters, pen-and-ink sketches, water-colours, and other memorabilia.

EDITOR'S PREFACE

Peter Thorogood is a leading authority on the life and work of Thomas Hood – indeed, his library at St Mary's House, Bramber, contains the largest collection in private hands of books by and about Thomas Hood. In the years leading up to 2018, Peter had completed an outline biography. However, by the time I began work on preparing this book for publication, Peter in his 97th year was unfortunately suffering from deteriorating eyesight, and it became clear that he would be unable to make any specific contribution to this project. So I had the challenge of undertaking the completion of this important book, while at the same time being sure to capture the essence of Peter's knowledge and expertise.

In addition to the outline biography, there was a typescript containing various chapters on an analysis of Hood's work, which Peter had worked on in the 1960s, long before the days of personal computers. Secondly, a book entitled *Development of the English Book Trade, 1700-1899*, edited by Robin Myers (a good friend of Peter's) and Michael Harris, included a chapter contributed by Peter on 'Thomas Hood: A Nineteenth Century Author and his Relations with the Book Trade to 1835'. The third additional source was a brief resumé of Hood's life written as an introduction to a book Peter published in 1995, *Thomas Hood – Poems Comic and Serious*, a selection of Hood's poetry.

My task, then, was to use Peter's biography, which already existed on computer, as a framework, and to merge in material from the other three sources. I also was able to benefit from four additional, and uniquely important, sources, all of which I was able to borrow from Peter's extensive library. These were, namely: *The Memorials of Thomas Hood*, collected and arranged by his daughter, Frances Freeling Broderip, with notes by his son, Tom; Hood's own *Literary Reminiscences*; the excellent *Letters of Thomas Hood*, edited and annotated by Peter Morgan; and *The Complete Poetical Works of Thomas Hood*, edited by Walter Jerrold. These four books were a veritable treasure trove. There was more treasure to be found in Peter's Thomas Hood collection – water colours, engravings, and humorous pen-and-ink sketches, all by Thomas Hood, and all material which has never before been published. I have used a selection of these as illustrations.

This book is in two parts: Part 1 is Hood's life and work, and Part 2 is a commentary on Hood's masterful caricature *The Progress of Cant*. It has been Peter's desire for many years to publish his analysis of Hood's famous engraving for a wider audience. It was first presented as a research paper at King's College, London, and printed in a collection of *Papers in Research and Criticism* in 1976. It is gratifying to now be able to include Peter's research paper in this book as, like many of Hood's poems, the engraving provides a fascinating insight into the social and political life of the 1820s.

Before I started work on this project, my knowledge of Hood began (and ended) with having to learn his poem *I Remember* at school. Not having any literary training, I have not ventured in any way to alter or enlarge on any critical analysis by Peter of Hood's poems, or indeed of his engraving. Rather, I have concentrated on adding, where appropriate, details, including anecdotes, about Hood's life, and checking the references, in particular the extracts from Hood's many letters. In this project, I have been ably assisted by my wife Diana, who has meticulously checked through the various iterations of the text numerous times for typographical and grammatical errors.

It has been a fascinating journey for me, in the process enlarging my hitherto scanty knowledge of Thomas Hood and the society of which he was a part. My hope is that this book does justice to Peter's authoritative work on Thomas Hood, which has been for him a lifetime's passion.

Alan Durden

CONTENTS

PART ONE

THOMAS HOOD –

HIS LIFE AND TIMES

Chapter 1 - The Age of Transition 1770-1840

'Rousseau, Sir, is a very bad man. I would sooner sign a sentence for his transportation, than that of any felon who has gone from the Old Bailey these many years.' Reported by Boswell in February 1776, this was Samuel Johnson's verdict on a man whose philosophy was to have a profound impact on European civilisation. Rousseau's ideas helped to unleash a violence so great as to destroy the old hierarchical coalitions and free them from bondage. Yet he was not a man of violence, rather a modernist, offering a new approach to education, a sentimentalist who could amuse himself by watching his tears fall into the waters of a lake, a man of simple tastes who believed that happiness consisted of 'a loyal friend, a loving wife, a cow and a little boat'. He advocated a 'higher sensibility' that foreshadowed profound changes in the intellectual, emotional and creative aspects of man's nature.

Reason was about to give way to violence and revolution, shedding not only tears but blood as the connotations of 'sense' and 'reason' burst beyond their classical definitions. Rousseau's loss of faith in what was then defined as 'sensibility' and his anti-intellectualism unwittingly nurtured seeds of anarchy. Natural emotions, untrammelled by reason and shorn of restricting influences of dogma and authoritarianism, expressed themselves in impassioned revolutionary ideals and the terror of the guillotine. The Noble Savage was divested of his nobility. 'Sensibility' had once referred to the degree to which a person could feel; now it came to mean the speed with which a person could respond to experience and be touched by the pathetic. Samuel Johnson had foreseen the danger and had described it as 'that hunger of the imagination which preys incessantly on life'. From this came a revival of medievalism, a love of Gothic ruins and a desire to improve nature's mistakes by wonders of landscape gardening and artificial follies.

Between the French Revolution of 1789 and the Battle of Waterloo in 1815 the face of England changed. Rousseau believed that the freedom of natural man had been destroyed by civilisation and that, though society may have been enriched by progress and invention, individual goodness had deteriorated. The growth of industry in England had created an inefficient and undisciplined economy, dangerous new machinery, gruesome accidents, pitiful working conditions in factories, starvation wages and the squalor of back-to-back dwellings. Keats wrote despairingly of the 'city's din'. It was an age of striking contrasts: of sophistication and savagery: whilst the children of the rich played in the elegant, manicured Regency London squares, the children of poor in the coal pits of the north of England were shackled to iron girdles for 16 hours a day to bring up coal to feed the voracious furnaces of the 'dark Satanic Mills' above ground. No 'Countenance Divine' shone forth upon their clouded hills. William Blake's vision of those horrors was powerfully echoed in Elizabeth Barrett Browning's memorable lines from *The Cry of the Children*:

> Do you hear the children weeping, O my brothers,
> Ere the sorrow comes with years?
> They are leaning their young heads against their mothers,
> And that cannot stop their tears.... [1]

A resultant surge of inventive energy encouraged industrialists to make more and more goods for markets at home and abroad, and, because of a subsequent expansion of trade, the great void between the aristocratic, governing and professional classes and the working class was gradually filled by the new middle class whose materialism became the backbone of Victorian England. By the end of the 19th century this class had become the dominant force in English society.

Romantic literature, though not altogether giving up classical principles of proportion, restraint and simplicity, turned more to the imagination and to visions of picturesque and grotesque aspects of life. Thus, although some lesser writers brought the Romantic Movement into disrepute by corrupting neo-Gothic literature, poets such as Wordsworth found ways to incorporate classical simplicity, believing that poetry should not be a spontaneous effusion of spirit but 'emotion recollected in tranquillity'.

Through this transformation, 18th-century canons were not given up but refashioned: sentiment was swollen into sentimentality; fancy ripened into imagination and wit dampened into whimsy and pathos.

For English Romantics, imagination had a particular attachment to reality and truth. Blake had taken visible objects and related them to the universal to achieve a visionary quality in poetry:

> To see a World in a Grain of Sand
>   And Heaven in a Wild Flower,
> Hold Infinity in the palm of your hand
>   And Eternity in an Hour.

Keats too, with his concept 'beauty is truth, truth beauty', achieved a subtle balance between the pangs of the 'wakeful anguish of the soul' and the almost pantheistic solace found in the beauty of nature:

> But when the melancholy fit shall fall
> Sudden from heaven like a weeping cloud,

That fosters the droop-headed flowers all,
And hides the green hill in an April shroud;
Then glut thy sorrow on a morning rose,
Or on the rainbow of the salt sand-wave,
Or on the wealth of globed peonies;
Or if thy mistress some rich anger shows,
Emprison her soft hand, and let her rave,
And feed deep, deep upon her peerless eyes.

This marriage of truth and imagination was followed by yet another element in the creation of poetry – colloquial idiom. In 1798, Wordsworth had expressed a wish 'to ascertain how far the language of conversation in the middle and lower classes of society could be adapted to the purposes of poetical pleasure'. In the hands of great poets such as Browning, the colloquial idiom could add to poetry's power and persuasion, but with minor writers it gave rise to unprecedented prolixity and encouraged the output of vast quantities of inferior prose and verse. In satire and caricature, inventiveness and facetiousness, combined with everyday idiom, produced a new kind of humour that became a true expression of the popular muse.

With the rise of the middle classes came a new set of values. Excess displays of emotion resulting from temper or temperament came to be regarded as vulgar. A reaction to the excesses of Byron and Shelley produced a general distrust of literature and forced on it an artificial purity that fostered hypocrisy, cant and a distortion of truth.

Another serious effect of the Industrial Revolution, especially during the 1820s, was an increase in sexual vice. Sensitivity to explicit sexual detail led to contempt for, and shame of, the human body. Increasing popularity of evangelical religion and fear of the underworld persuaded the middle classes that life must centre on the home. Thus Tennyson refers to Queen Victoria as 'Mother, wife and Queen' in that order. In 1818, Thomas Bowdler had published *a Family Shakespeare* in which 'nothing is added to the original text, but those words and expressions omitted which cannot with propriety be read aloud in a family'. The Victorian house, with its Gothic exterior (in pale imitation of Venice), its aspidistra, its horsehair chairs, its antimacassars, its Christmas tree newly imported from the continent, its musical evenings and its gargantuan supper parties, became a temple of purity where children remained untainted by the corruption of the adult world. They were to be seen but not heard and quietly peruse their Annuals or listen to Father reading from the works of the 'ethereal' Felicia Hemans - all amid the plush and bric-à-brac of a Victorian drawing room. In spite of this, life was overshadowed by the humourless Puritanism of the Lutheran Prince Consort and clouded by suppressed emotion and a struggle for respectability.

In this age of extremes, faith and scepticism, poverty and great material wealth, maudlin sentimentality and a dogged determinism could exist side by side as expressions of the same moral code that fostered both idealism and hypocrisy. New words crept into the language: at a meeting of the Preston Temperance Society in 1833 a Mr Turner asserted that nothing but 't-t-total' would do (thus 'teetotal'), homes grew 'snug' and 'cosy', while opinions based on moral abstractions became increasingly 'smug' as the century proceeded. The Romantic paradox of blood and sensibility was replaced by the Victorian dilemma of universal opposites sharing a context. A veil of deep complacency covered society and truth became confused with morality: 'It is right, therefore it is true'. Subsequently idealism caused further confusion.

In the age of Freese Green's photography, literature gained some of the clarity and precision of science. Detailed delineation of visible objects produced poetry such as Tennyson's *The Shell*:

> See what a lovely shell,
> Small and pure as a pearl,
> Lying close to my foot,
> Frail but a work divine,
> Made so fairly well
> With delicate spire and whorl
> How exquisitely minute
> A miracle of design.

With their attention to detailed description and their propensity for complex analysis, the Victorians wrote copiously, churning out vast quantities of poetry, political and religious tracts, lengthy novels, ponderous verse-dramas and voluminous diaries. Great emphasis was attached to 'the importance of being earnest', later to be brilliantly satirised by Oscar Wilde. It was this earnestness, allied to idealism and endeavour that filled them to overflowing with the correctness of their material progress and urged them to think, write and behave philanthropically. Thomas Carlyle cried out his watchwords of work, courage and truth. Thousands attended Sunday religious meetings, sang with the Salvation Army, helped the poor, made contributions to charity, endowed schools and hospitals. They wrote novels such as those by Dickens and Disraeli, revealing the plight of the poverty-stricken labouring classes, or – like Ebenezer Elliott, Elizabeth Barrett Browning and Thomas Hood – made poignant and persuasive poetic pleas for justice and mercy. Gradually, with the rise of the 'Victorian Conscience', other writers and thinkers began to speak eloquently of the barely perceptible tensions that lay below the surface of society, revealing the dangers of deeply rooted class differences which, if not understood, might lead to serious economic and social instability.

Between the death of Byron in 1824 and the publication of Browning's *Dramatic Lyrics* in 1842, the English literary scene suffered a poetic lull. Coleridge and Wordsworth had given up writing, though Robert Southey (Poet-Laureate), Samuel Rogers, George Darley, Ebenezer Elliott, Thomas Beddoes and L.E.L. (Letitia Elizabeth Landon) were widely read but, as Beddoes remarked in 1824:

> The disappearance of Shelley seems to have been followed
> by instant darkness and owl-season; whether the vociferous
> Darley is to be the comet or tender-faced L.E.L. the milk
> and watery moon of our darkness are questions for the
> astrologers.

The greater works of Browning and Tennyson were still to appear, but it was another poet, Thomas Hood (until then known only as the sub-editor of the *London Magazine*) who emerged with comics and lyrics that satisfied popular taste for wit and humour, tinged with the grotesque and the pathetic.

Engraving of Windsor Castle by Thomas Hood

Chapter 2 - The Early Years

Thomas Hood was born on 23 May 1799 in London, within the sound of Bow Bells. A 'blue plaque' on the wall of what was once the site of 31, The Poultry, now commemorates the event. His birth, however, was not registered until 27 November 1817, presumably the birth certificate being needed to register for an apprenticeship. His father had left his native Carse of Gowrie to travel south to London, where – by his Scottish tenacity and industry – he eventually became a partner in the publishers Vernor and Hood of 31 The Poultry, in the City of London. In collaboration with John Britton[*], and the engravers, John and Henry Le Keux[†], he published successful topographical works, and with encouragement from Capel Lofft[‡], the verses of the 'picturesque' poets, Henry Kirke White[§] and Robert Bloomfield[**]. Although said to have written two novels, Thomas Hood senior's most notable contribution to publishing was that he encouraged trade with America after the loss of the colonies in 1776. He married Elizabeth Sands, daughter of engraver James Sands and brought up a large family of two sons and four daughters.[††] It appears that he was extremely fond of his elder son, James, whom he undoubtedly hoped would succeed him in the business. It also seems likely that, with all the cares of the book trade on his shoulders, he was in the habit of leaving his sickly younger son, Thomas, to the affectionate attentions of Mrs Hood.

The family home in The Poultry, only a stone's throw from the Mansion House and St Paul's Cathedral, was a busy thoroughfare of noise and bustle which could hardly have suited a sensitive child. In 1807, however, when Hood was eight years old, the growing family moved to a larger house in the country. In those days, Islington was a quiet village on the edge of the City, and it was there, at 5 Lower Street, an old Queen Anne house on the

---

[*] John Britton (1771-1857) Art historian, architectural historian, topographer.

[†] John Le Keux (1783-1846) Engraver, specialist in architectural engraving, and father of engraver and illustrator John Henry Le Keux (1812-96); Henry Le Keux (1787-1868), engraver.

[‡] Capel Lofft (1751-1824) was a British lawyer, write and amateur astronomer. He became patron of Robert Bloomfield, and arranged for the publication of the latter's *The Farmer's Boy*.

[§] Henry Kirke White (1785-1806) was an English poet and hymn-writer. He died at the young age of 21.

[**] Robert Bloomfield (1766-1823) was an English working-class poet. The poem that made his reputation was *The Farmer's Boy*.

[††] The children of Thomas Hood (senior) and Elizabeth Sands: sons James and Thomas; daughters Elizabeth (Betsy), Anne, Jessie and Catherine.

green, that the growth of the young poet's mind began to bear fruit. It was this house, rather than his birthplace in The Poultry, that he affectionately recalls in his now famous poem, *I Remember*.

To escape from the noise and bustle of the city into the comparatively rural setting of Islington village was, for the poet, not to be born, but reborn. The 'roses, red and white', the 'lilacs where the robin built', and the 'fir trees dark and high' must have seemed to the imaginative child the attributes of paradise, with heaven never very far away, Images of childhood appear in Hood's poems and woodcuts throughout his life. His wistful excursions into the halcyon days of childhood are almost invariably tempered with regret at the passing of innocence and beauty. Indeed, each verse of *I Remember* ends on a darker, brooding note which foreshadows the bitter experiences that life had yet in store for him.

We have to rely with some degree of uncertainty on the *Literary Reminiscences* for any details we possess of the poet Hood's life at this time, but we can fairly assume that he had become quite familiar with the world of books and booksellers from the earliest years of his infancy spent in The Poultry. That first view of country life at Islington, however, was to be one of the strongest of the early influences on his poetry.

He was proud of being a Cockney and wrote in his *Literary Reminiscences*:

> Next to being a citizen of the world, it must be the best
> thing to be born a citizen of the world's greatest city…a
> literary man should exult rather than otherwise that he first
> saw the light – or perhaps the fog – in the same metropolis
> as Milton, Gray, De Foe, Pope, Byron, Lamb, and other
> town-born authors.[2]

I REMEMBER, I REMEMBER

I remember, I remember,
The house where I was born,
The little window where the sun
Came peeping in at morn;
He never came a wink too soon,
Nor brought too long a day,
But now, I often wish the night
Had borne my breath away!

I remember, I remember,
The roses, red and white,
The violets, and the lily-cups,
Those flowers made of light!
The lilacs where the robin built,
And where my brother set
The laburnum on his birthday, -
The tree is living yet!

I remember, I remember,
Where I used to swing,
And thought the air must rush as fresh
To swallows on the wing;
My spirit flew in feathers then,
That is so heavy now,
And summer pools could hardly cool
The fever at my brow!

I remember, I remember,
The fir trees dark and high;
I used to think their slender tops
Were close against the sky:
It was a childish ignorance,
But now 'tis little joy
To know I'm farther off from heav'n
Than when I was a boy.

Hood was described by James Hessey, a friend of his father, as 'a singular child, silent and retired, with much quiet humour and apparently delicate in health'. At school, Hood appears to have had a repugnance for things mathematical and geographical, and possessed a natural inclination towards the niceties of grammar. 'I was,' he tells us in his *Literary Reminiscences*, 'sufficiently at home (during the vacations) in the quibbles of English grammar to bore all my parents, relations, friends and acquaintances…' He modestly admits, in a throwaway sort of manner, that he won a Latin prize, and that his indulgences in the pleasure of literature led him into trouble on at least one occasion when, being 'too fond of his book' (Robinson Crusoe), he was severely punished for reading it during the lesson. At home, at least, he could enjoy the pleasures of browsing in family library, perhaps reading works published by his father's firm such as Anstey's *New Bath Guide*, Robert Bloomfield's *The Farmer's Boy* or Henry Kirke White's *Clifton Grove*.

From an early age he loved practical-joking and could turn sadness into humour and serious remarks into witticisms. As a boy, the only person he ever frightened by a practical joke was himself. Having traced a diabolical face on the ceiling of the passage outside his bedroom to frighten his brother as he came up to bed, he forgot what he had done and, coming to bed early himself, he was so frightened by the phantom of his own making that he fled down the stairs in his nightshirt and burst into a drawing-room crowded with his father's guests.

His early education was gained at a Dame school, run by two maiden ladies called Hogsflesh, whose establishment was at Tokenhouse Yard in Moorgate. From there, at the age of nine, he was removed to a seminary at Islington and thence, as a boarder, to Alfred House Academy for Young Gentlemen in Camberwell Green. run by Dr Nicholas Wanostrocht. His remembrance of the school in his *Ode on a Distant Prospect of Clapham Academy* is expressed in mock-nostalgic vein (with echoes of Gray's *Ode on a Distant Prospect of Eton College*):

> Ah me! those old familiar bounds!
> That classic house, those classic grounds,
>   My pensive thought recalls!
> What tender urchins now confine,
> What little captives now repine,
>   Within yon irksome walls?
> There I was birch'd, there I was bred!
> There like a little Adam fed
> From Learning's woeful tree!
> The weary tasks I used to con −
> The hopeless leaves I wept upon! −
> Most fruitless leaves to me![3]

Interestingly, among former pupils of the school were the brothers James and Horace Smith, who would have been there some years before Hood, later becoming part of Hood's social circle. They became well known for their *Rejected Addresses*, parodies of established writers of the day. Their publication was occasioned by the competition for an address to be read at the formal opening of the rebuilt Theatre Royal, Drury Lane, after the disastrous fire of 1809.

He elaborates on his experience in *Literary Reminiscences*:

> In this ignorant world, where we proverbially live and learn, we may indeed leave off school, but our education terminates with life itself....From the preparatory school, I was transplanted in due time to what was called by courtesy, a finishing one, where I was immediately set to begin everything from the beginning. As this was but a backward way of coming forward, there seemed little chance of my ever becoming what Mrs Malaprop calls "a progeny of learning"; indeed my education was pursued very much after the plan laid by that feminine authority. I had nothing to do with Hebrew, or Algebra, or Simony, or Fluxions, or Paradoxes, or with such inflammatory branches; but I obtained a supercilious knowledge of accounts, with enough geometry to make me acquainted with the contagious countries. ...[4]

Sometime in 1811, his brother James, showing early signs of consumption, was sent to his uncle Robert Sands, in Sandhurst, Berkshire, for a change of air. While there, he fell mortally ill. When the elder Hood heard the news, he rushed to his ailing son's bedside, forsaking his business and all else besides. On his return, Mr Hood caught a violent cold from riding home outside the coach; or perhaps it was that he contracted his son's illness. But whatever the cause of his own subsequent illness, he sickened rapidly and predeceased his ailing son by four months, dying on 20 August.

The publishing house of Vernor and Hood went into liquidation, and Hood's bereaved mother Elizabeth and her family of five children now found themselves in very straitened circumstances to face an uncertain future. Hood was sent to a poorer school, located over a grocer's shop – indicating a reduction in the family finances: 'What might have been called a High School in reference to its distance from the ground.' There, he says:

> I picked up some Latin, was a tolerable English Grammarian, and so good a French scholar, that I earned a

few guineas – my first literary fee - by revising a new edition of 'Paul et Virginie,' for the press.[5]

The school, however, was not prospering, as the number were falling. But one morning the school assumed a new role in the history of co-education, as the boys witnessed the arrival of a girl pupil, complete with bag and books, causing unprecedented consternation among the angelic host. Thus:

> Of course SHE instantly formed a class; and had any form SHE might prefer to herself:- the most of us being just old enough to resent what was considered as an affront on the corduroy sex, and just young enough to be beneath any gallantry to the silken one. The truth was that there was a plan for translating us, and turning the unsuccessful Boys' School into a Ladies' Academy… A brief period only had elapsed, when, lo! A leash of female school *Fellows* – three sisters, like the degrees of comparison personified, Big, Bigger and Biggest – made their unwelcome appearance, and threatened to push us from our stools. They were greeted, accordingly, with all the annoyances that juvenile malice could suggest. It is amusing, yet humiliating, to remember the nuisances the sex endured at the hands of those who were thereafter to honour the shadow of its shoe-tie, to groan, moan, sigh, and sicken for its smiles – to become poetical, prosaical, nonsensical, lack-a-daisical, and perhaps even melodramatical for its sake. Numberless were the desk-quakes, the ink-spouts, the book-bolts, the pea-showers, and other unregistered phenomena, which likened the studies of those four unhappy maidens to the 'Pursuit of Knowledge under Difficulties,' – so that it glads me to reflect, that I was in a very small minority against the persecution; having already begun to read poetry, and even write something which was egregiously mistaken for something of the same nature.[6]

In *A Retrospective Review*, he looks back to these innocent schooldays with a nostalgic sense of loss:

> No skies so blue or so serene,
> As then; – no leaves look half so green
> As cloth'd the play-ground tree!
> All things I lov'd are alter'd so,

Nor does it ease my heart to know
That change resides in me![7]

By the time Hood was 12 years of age, he was an avid reader of poetry and was beginning to write his own poetry. Robert Bloomfield's *The Farmer's Boy* was a particular inspiration. This poem, which follows the seasonal pattern of rural life as seen through the life of Giles, a young shepherd, was published, as we have noted, by Hood's father's firm, Vernor & Hood, in 1800. It was a phenomenal success, selling over 26,000 copies in the first three years. A combination of 'Feeling, Piety, poetic imagery and Animation, a taste for the picturesque, a true sense of the natural and pathetic, force of thought, and liveliness of imagination', the poem was the expression of 'simplicity, sweetness and tenderness', as celebrated in the *Eclogues* of Virgil:

> Neglected now the early daisy liest
> Nor thou, pale primrose, bloom'st the only prize:
> Advancing SPRING profusely spreads abroad
> Flow'rs of all hues, with sweetest fragrance stor'd;
> Where'r she treads, LOVE gladdens every plain,
> Delight of tiptoe bears her lucid train...

It is easy to see the attractions of such gentle verses as these on the mind of the young Thomas Hood, eager for 'simplicity', sweetness and tenderness', qualities to be found in an unpublished sonnet of his, the first two lines of which are a translation straight from Virgil:

> Look how a slender rivulet steals along,
> In windings devious, through a meadow's grass;
> Its waters all too scant to yield a song
> Of murmur'd pleasure unto those who pass;
> Therefore, with lowly aim, it does but seek
> The thirsty herbage to refresh unseen;
> Whereat each tiny leaf, and flow'ret meek
> Doth clothe itself with sweets, and livelier green.
> So the True Heart who has not store of wealth
> His poorer brethren to endow withal,
> Doeth his gentle acts of good by stealth,
> That so the World may not perceive at all:
> Nor should we know that virtue which he hath
> Save for the brightening looks that mark his humble path.

In later years, when he was writing the verses for Tylney Hall, Hood recalled the theme and mood of his earlier sonnet in 'Still glides the gentle streamlet on':

STILL GLIDES THE GENTLE STREAMLET

Still glides the gentle streamlet on,
With shifting current new and strange;
The water that was here is gone,
But those green shadows do not change.

Serene, or ruffled by the storm,
On present waves as on the past,
The mirrored grave retains its form,
The self-same trees their semblance cast.

The hue each fleeting globule wears,
That drop bequeaths it to the next,
One picture still the surface bears,
To illustrate the murmured text.

So, love, however time may flow,
Fresh hours pursuing those that flee
One constant image still shall show
My tide of life is true to thee!

There is an echo, too, in this poem of Wordsworth's lines 'Still glides the Stream, and shall for ever glide', which suggests that, as might be expected with any young poet, Hood was in a strongly assimilative phase of his development in the early 1820s. Whilst writing poetry which was by no means second-rate, his inspiration was at this time largely second-hand, the product of his extensive reading from earlier periods.

***

When Hood was 14 years old, he completed his schooling, and it seemed pretty clear to Mrs. Hood that she would have to find her remaining son a place in the City until such time as he could decide on a suitable career for himself. Parodying Anne Hunter's words to Joseph Haydn's well-known song, 'My mother bids me bind my hair', Hood entertains us with a catalogue of undesirable occupations:

> My mother bids me bind my heir,
> But not the trade where I should bind;
> To place a boy – the how and where –
> It is the plague of parent-kind!
>
> She does not hint the slightest plan,
> Nor what indentures to indorse;
> Whether to bind him to a man, –
> Or, like Mazeppa, to a horse.

Should he join the Stock Exchange? Should he become a statesman? A tailor?

> A Seedsman? – I'd not have him so;
> A Grocer's plum might disappoint;
> A Butcher? – no, not that – although
> I hear 'the times are out of joint'!

Many are the trades to choose from. A hardware dealer? A soldier or sailor? A hairdresser? A joiner? A churchman? A publisher?

> Dresser of hair? – that's not the sort;
> A Joiner jars with his desire –
> A Churchman? – James is very short,
> And cannot to a church aspire.
>
> A Lawyer? – that's a hardish term!
> A Publisher might give him ease,

25

If he could into Longman's firm,
Just plunge at once 'in medias Rees'.

After rejecting the idea of a builder, a coppersmith, a publican, a paper-maker, a miller, an undertaker ('one of those/That do not hope to get their living!'), an auctioneer ('obliged to do as he is bid!'), a cooper, a fishmonger, a painter and a glazier, among other trades and professions, he comes to no great conclusion:

Well, something must be done! to look
On all my little works around –
James is too big a boy, like book
To leave upon the shelf unbound.

But what to do? – my temples ache
From evening's dew till morning's pearl,
What course to take my boy to make –
O could I make my boy – a girl!

Mrs Hood's attempts to bind her son in apprenticeship to some profession or other were constantly foiled by the boy's ill health; a very serious attack of scarlet fever incapacitated him for a long time, undermining his youthful energies and holding up the natural growth of mind and body. The sick child naturally clings to the love of she who nurses and soothes his pains more readily than does a healthy child, and through his constant ill health Hood formed a strong emotional attachment to his mother. When his mother died some years later, when Hood was about 22, he felt the loss, not only of a mother, but a close friend and counsellor, more deeply than would a normal healthy young man. His emotional vulnerability remained with him for the rest of his life, obviated in later years by a capable and loving wife, eight years his senior, who could carry him through crisis after crisis.

Eventually, through the help of a family friend, sometime in 1814 the young Thomas Hood found himself perched on a counting-house stool in a shipping firm called Bell & Company, a firm of importers in the Russian trade. 'The principal of our firm…had a turn for Belles Lettres, and would have winked with both eyes at verses which did not intrude or confuse their figures with those in the Ledger.'[8] It was patently clear that his love of literature was stronger than his love of ledgers, as we can see from the wry sonnet he wrote some twenty years later:

Time was, I sat upon a lofty stool,
At lofty desk, and with a clerkly pen,

26

Began each morning, at the stroke of ten,
To write in Bell & Co's commercial school;
In Warnford Court, a shady nook and cool,
The favourite retreat of merchant men;
Yet would my quill turn vagrant even then,
And take stray dips in the Castilian pool.
Now double entry − now a flowery trope −
Mingling poetic honey with trade wax −
Blogg brothers − Milton − Grote and Prescott − Pope −
Bristles – and Hogg – Glyn and Halifax –
Rogers – and Towgood – Hemp – the Bard of Hope –
Barilla – Byron – Tallow – Burns – and Flax! …[9]

It was not long before ill health intervened and cut short his stay with the firm of 'Bell & Co.' A distaste for ledgers and accounting remained with Hood for the rest of his life; ironically, this was to lead him into placing his trust in the hands of the untrustworthy on many occasions in later years. But now, in 1815, he was young and green and full of hopes for the future. It was a time of victory and rejoicing. Napoleon had been defeated. The sea lanes were free once more. With no profession decided upon just yet, Mrs Hood arranged for her son to stay with relatives in Dundee. The hope was that his congenitally weak heart and lungs would strengthen in the crisp air of Scotland, and his health would benefit from having ample time for reading and writing. So it was that, soon after the Battle of Waterloo, he sailed down the Thames on the trading vessel *Union* for the long four-day sea voyage to Dundee. On arrival he saw, in the days before railways and mechanised means of communication, a town untouched by the revolutionary technology of the country's new industrial cities.

His visit of a few weeks became one of two years. He stayed initially with his maternal aunt, Jean Keay, then moved on to the boarding house of one of her friends, a Mrs Butterworth. It was from Dundee that Hood wrote to his aunt in London thanking her for a present she had sent him and enclosing 116 lines of a satirical poem in the style of Christopher Anstey's *New Bath Guide*, entitled *Dundee Guide*. Anstey's sprightly anapaests are well-displayed in a passage comparing the city of Bath with its neighbouring towns:

Of all the gay places the world can afford,
By gentle and simple for pastime ador'd
Fine balls, and fine concerts, fine buildings and springs,
Fine walks, and fine views, and a thousand fine things,
(Not to mention the sweet situation and air)
What place, my dear mother, with Bath compare?

Let Bristol for commerce and dirt be renown'd;
At Sal'sbury pen-knives and scissors be ground;
The towns of Devizes, of Bradford, and Frome,
May boast that they better can manage the loom;
I believe that they may; – but the world to refine
In manners, in dress, in politeness to shine,
O Bath! Let the art, let the glory be thine!

Hood's portrait of Dundee, a parody of Anstey's poem, is less flattering:

The town is ill-built, and is dirty beside
For with water it's scantily, badly supplied
By wells, where the servants, in filling their pails,
Stand for hours, spreading scandal, and falsehoods and tales.
And abounds so in smells that a stranger supposes
The people are very deficient in noses.
Their buildings, as though they'd been scanty of ground,
Are crammed into corners that cannot be found.
Or as though so ill built and contrived they had been,
That the town were ashamed they should ever be seen.
And their rooted dislike and aversion to waste
Is suffer'd sometimes to encroach on their taste,
For beneath a Theatre or Chapel they'll pop
A sale room, a warehouse, or mean little shop,
Whose windows, or rather no windows at all,
Are more like to so many holes in the wall.
And four churches together, with only one steeple,
Is an emblem quite apt of the thrift of the people.[10]

While the poem is an immature piece, it shows real verve and youthful confidence, revealing an early tendency to satirise society, manners and customs. His melodramatic verse-narrative *The Bandit*[11] was also written at this time, showing his debt to 18th century satirists and his love for Gothic subjects in Byronic style, though it also lacks as yet a sure grasp of his material. It was at Dundee too that he read the poetry of Robert Burns, Allan Ramsey and Allan Cunningham and basked in 'the contemplative quiet, the sweet wholesome country air and the picturesque scenery.'

Hood never lost a good opportunity to comment in verse or prose on any contemporary publication that took his fancy. A fine example is to be found in his comic poem 'Our Village', which parodies Mary Russell Mitford's literary sketches of rural life, the first of which was published in 1824. Mitford's *Our Village* describes people, places, pastimes and customs in and around her village of Three Mile Cross in Hampshire:

A little world of our own, close packed and insulated like ants in an ant-hill, or bees in a hive, or sheep in a fold, or nuns in a convent, or sailors on a ship; where we know everyone, are known to everyone, interested in everyone, and are authorised to hope that everyone feels an interest in us.

Hood's fine satirical evocation of this haven of rural felicity begins thus:

> Our village, that's to say not Miss Mitford's village, but our village of Bullock Smithy,
> Is come into by an avenue of trees, three oak pollards, two elders and a withy;
> And in the middle, there's a green of about not exceeding an acre and a half;
> It's common to all, and fed off by nineteen cows, six ponies, three horses, five asses, two foals, seven pigs, and a calf!
> Besides a pond in the middle, as is held by a similar sort of common law lease,
> And contains twenty ducks, six drakes, three ganders, two dead dogs, four drown'd kittens, and twelve geese.
> Of course the green's cropt very close, and does famous for bowling when the village boys play at cricket;
> Only some horse, or pig, or cow, or great jackass, is sure to come and stand right before the wicket.
> There's fifty-five private houses, let alone barns and workshops, and pigstyes, and poultry huts, and such-like sheds;
> With plenty of public-houses – two Foxes, one Green Man, three Bunch of Grapes, one Crown and six King's Heads.

THE LADY OF "OUR VILLAGE."

29

At Dundee, he indulged in open-air pursuits such as trout fishing:

> I haunted the banks and braes, or paid flying visits to the
> burns, with a rod intended to punish that rising generation
> amongst fishes called trout. But I whipped in vain. Trout
> there were in plenty, but like obstinate double teeth, with a
> bad operator, they would neither be pulled out nor come
> out of themselves.[12]

Nevertheless, he was able to enjoy 'the contemplative quiet, the sweet
wholesome country air and the picturesque scenery'. He also sailed on the
River Tay, learning the rudiments of boat-craft sufficient for 'taking the
helm without either going too near the wind or too distant from the port'.
He occasionally found himself 'entrusted with the guidance of the Coach-
Boat – so-called from its carrying the passengers by the Edinburgh Mail –
particularly in a calm, when the utmost exertions of the crew were required
at the oars'. On one such voyage, he records a memorable incident. One of
the passengers was carrying a rather lively turtle, and for some reason
thought that it would benefit from a dip in the sea. On lifting it over the
side, the creature began to struggle so violently that its owner had to let it
go, tumbling backwards into the boat suddenly bereaved of his precious
turtle.[13]

Sometime in the autumn of 1817, Hood was thought well enough to
return to London, secure in the knowledge that his mother had found a
solution to the problem of which of the many trades and professions might
prove best suited to a young man of weak constitution. He was placed this
time with his maternal uncle, the distinguished topographical engraver,
Robert Sands, whose country home was in Berkshire. The young Hood had
already spent much of his childhood in drawing and sketching, and now
resumed his artistic endeavours.

Rural Scene – Berkshire Downs, by Thomas Hood

In *The Progress of Art*, Hood takes a wistful look back to his first art lessons when he abandoned crayon and chalk for the more adventurous Indian Ink and water-colour:

> Oh then, what black Mont Blancs arose,
> Crested with soot and not with snows;
> What clouds of dingy hue!
> In spite of what the Bard has penned,
> I fear the distance did not 'lend
> Enchantment to the view'.
>
> But colours came! – like morning light,
> With gorgeous hues replacing night,
> Or Spring's enlivened scene;
> At once the sable shades withdrew;
> My skies got very, very blue;
> My trees extremely green.

A track through the woods, by Thomas Hood

The brief spell in the quiet of the Berkshire Downs, provided the romantic young artist with picturesque subjects for some charming sketches and water-colours. Soon, he had acquired sufficient technique to be accepted to study engraving with the brothers John and Henry Le Keux, at which time he did an engraving of St. Cleron's, Galway, for J. P. Neale's work on country houses. His health had vastly improved, and he now felt able to apply for an apprenticeship. He began working on an instrument for copying drawings, which he presented to the Society of Arts for approval, but the application was unsuccessful. As for poetry: 'I cannot find time to write such things now – and, indeed, after the study and close application necessary in engraving, it would cease to be any relaxation'. In a letter to his Dundee friend, George Rollo, Hood wrote:

> …I am now obliged to turn the amusing, if I can, to the profitable, not that I am ambitious, or of a very money loving disposition, but I am obliged to be so. Otherwise, I believe, if left to myself, I should be content with a very moderate station, for, like you, I believe I am of a 'domestic

indolent turn.' But this is all speculative reasoning, perhaps; and I might find – that summit attained – that the content was as far off as ever, increasing by a kind of arithmetical progression. Thus, when seen from the valley, the summit of the mountain appears to touch the skies; but when we have ascended and reached its top, we seem, and no doubt are, as far from heaven as ever!

a point which Hood poignantly makes in the last stanza of *I Remember*:

I remember, I remember,
The fir trees dark and high;
I used to think their slender tops
Were close against the sky;
It was a childish ignorance,
But now 'tis little joy,
To know I'm farther off from heav'n
Than when I was a boy.

Engraving by Thomas Hood of ducks on water

Engraving by Thomas Hood of a woodland scene

Chapter 3 - The London Magazine

By 1820, Hood had started to write poetry again, as well as working assiduously at his engraving. He began to compose a number of addresses and recitations for an enthusiastic group of young ladies. 'I continue to receive such pleasure from our literary society,' he wrote to his Dundee friend, George Rollo, 'and from my own pursuits in that way – in which, considering my little time, I am very industrious – that is to say, I spoil a deal of paper.' He reported that, besides a mock heroic love tale, he had lately finished 'two poetical addresses to the society on closing and opening a fresh session, with various pieces, chiefly amatory.' His enthusiasm seems to have continued unabated because, in June of the following year, he took along another Dundee friend, Andrew Wyllie, to hear his 'essay on Poetry to close the session.' This address was later reworked and published in the *London Magazine* in November 1821 as *The Departure of Summer*. It was a derivative piece, being a mixture of Milton, James Thomson, Leigh Hunt, and Keats, with touches here and there of Marvell's *Thoughts on a Garden*, Bolingbroke's speech before his exile in *Richard II*, and Shelley's *Ode to the West Wind*, for good measure. With the coming of winter, the poet grieves for the warm summer days that are past:

> Summer is gone on swallows' wings,
> And Earth has buried all her flowers:
> No more the lark, the linnet sings,
> But Silence sits in faded bowers.
> There is the shadow on the plain
> Of Winter ere he comes again, –
> There is in woods a solemn sound
> Of hollow warnings whisper'd round,
> As Echo in her deep recess
> For once had turned a prophetess.
> Shuddering Autumn stops to list,
> And breathes his fear in sudden sighs,
> With clouded face, and hazel eyes
> That quench themselves, and hide in mist.

These were the lines of a fledgling poet, who had only just been exposed to the wider world of poetry as a young greenhorn, but they no doubt impressed his respectful, perhaps even adoring female audience. Many of these literary societies would fail to survive, due to financial pressures placed on their organising committees. Although this would leave Hood with no outlet for public recitation, at least his early pieces were beginning to appear in the *London Magazine*.

Meanwhile, there was a controversy as to what had happened to the *Dundee Guide*, which had disappeared mysteriously, but Hood seemed to accept the loss with equanimity - probably because he had better things written and ready for publication. He mentioned in a letter to George Rollo in June 1821 that he 'would rather the *Dundee Guide* should remain unknown, for I think I can do better things'.

Quite suddenly he was beset by other problems, as his mother, Elizabeth Hood, died in July 1821, leaving him to run the Islington house and to look after his four sisters. He wrote to George Rollo in Dundee: 'I have suffered an inexpressible anguish of mind in parting from my only parent, and but for the consolations which I have had I should have sunk under it'.[14] His poem, *The Deathbed*, was thought to have been written in memory of his mother, though his son Tom Hood, writing later in the *Memorials of Thomas Hood*, suggested that it was written on the death of his sister, Ann. Whatever its origin, the poem has become one of the most popular inclusions in anthologies of English poetry. Few poets have recorded more poignantly such anguish and grief at bereavement as expressed by Hood in his poem:

> We watch'd her breathing through the night ,
> Her breathing soft and low,
> As in her breast the wave of life
> Kept heaving to and fro!
>
> So silently we seemed to speak −
> So slowly moved about!
> As we had lent her half our powers
> To eke her living out!
>
> Our very hopes belied our fears,
> Our fears our hopes belied −
> We thought her dying when she slept,
> And sleeping when she died!
>
> For when the morn came dim and sad −
> And chill with early showers,
> Her quiet eyelids closed − she had
> Another morn than ours! [15]

One of the most affecting letters Hood wrote at this time during July 1821 was to his father's friend and former assistant, John Taylor, now an established publisher:

> Had I been ever inclined to underrate acts of Friendship, the loss of my dear Father and the consequent tenour of my life would have taught me their full value; and indeed I have learned to feel the full force & worth of the least expressions and even looks of kindness. But in justice to my heart I must declare that without this experience and ever since the death of my brother, I have held you in affectionate remembrance – your kind attentions to him in his last days would have insured my eternal gratitude even had there been no happiness in loving one who was his Friend, nor any in the hope that I might inherit those mutual feelings which must have been as delightful to him as they are now to myself... When I tell you that your kindness contributed to soothe the last days of my dear Mother – that she mentioned your name amongst her last thoughts and desired me to make to you her acknowledgements... I have seen the end of the best of Mothers. She expired with her head upon my arm – her eyes burning towards me with their wonted fondness, till the Spirit which looked thro them was called away and dragging my arm from the lifeless weight it supported, I resigned my dear Mother for ever. It was a shock which in spite of long preparation was almost too much for me, & had it not been a release from a state of suffering and agony at times, would have been quite overwhelming. But I have no sorrow but for the loss of so much goodness and affection., & the regret that I may not nurse her & comfort her in a grey-haired age. I have had the consolation of being with her & performing all the little offices in my power, for her comfort, and I have received from her the last marks of affection which I can only deserve by the most affectionate regard to her memory and a warm and unceasing kindness to her orphan children. – My mind is recovering its composure, but I am rather unwell from the fatigue & agitation which I have undergone of late, and I think a cold which I have caught in sleeping in the next room to my dear Mother, with the window open. I have never felt such violent transitions from pain to pleasure as at the alternate, delirious & sensible intervals with my dear Mother. In the first she

could always recognise me but it was only in the last that with a feebler & calmer voice she resumed all her affection.[16]

In October he wrote to Rollo once more: 'I am engraving and writing prose and poetry by turns. I have some papers coming forth in next month's *London Magazine*, signed incog. And in the meantime I am busy extending and correcting my long poem and other pieces for publication'.

Keats had died the previous February and there is no doubt that Hood was affected by the tragedy, as he shared affinities with Keats in both his life and his work.

There were other influences too, for published around that time were the last cantos of Byron's *Childe Harold*, various essays by Charles Lamb, Mary Shelley's *Frankenstein*, Scott's *Heart of Midlothian* and, in 1819, Byron's *Don Juan*. William Cobbett was beginning to awaken interest in the neglected rural economy, while John Stuart Mill was developing his theories of political economy. England had now entered the reign of George IV and the *London Magazine* was at the height of its popularity, having among its contributors Charles Lamb, William Hazlitt, Allan Cunningham, Thomas Carlyle and Hood himself.

At this time certain differences came to a head between the *London Magazine* and *Blackwood's Magazine,* which subsequently led to a duel between the editor of the former, John Scott, and Jonathan Christie, who was a friend of John Gibson Lockhart of *Blackwood's*. Scott had vehemently attacked Lockhart in the pages of the *London* and the resulting bitterness between the two men over a period of six months grew out of all proportion. Defending the honour and name of his friend Lockhart, Christie challenged Scott to a duel, which took place on the night of 16 February 1821 at Chalk Farm. Scott was mortally wounded, though he lingered eleven days before he died. The need for a new editor of the *London Magazine* became urgent. The proprietors now found themselves in an awkward predicament and, in desperation, approached William Hazlitt, who declined their invitation. Some months elapsed and still no solution presented itself, the journal finally being sold to Taylor and Hessey in July 1821. John Taylor, who had gained valuable experience working with the family publishing firm, Vernor, Hood & Sharpe, became its editor. William Hazlitt was appointed dramatic critic, and Charles Lamb contributed regular articles under the pen-name, 'Elia'.

Taylor proved to be a man of taste and judgement and, in August 1820, had written of Hood to the elder Taylor at Retford: 'His talents are very good and he has written some clever things in prose and verse. It occurred to me that his help would relieve me of a good deal of the drudgery of revising MS etc. and when Hessey returns I will have some talk about it.'

The young Hood was promptly installed as a 'sort of sub-editor'. He was delighted to bid farewell to engraving and to indulge his talent for writing, for not only was he editing, accepting or rejecting articles for the Magazine, but he was also contributing articles himself.

But Taylor had nothing of the flair John Scott had shown as editor. He was often quarrelsome and hypersensitive to criticism. His habit of altering or 'improving' the manuscripts of his contributors without consultation did not endear him to them, and his reputation as the bowdleriser of Keats and Clare did not inspire confidence in his powers of editorship. Already by 1823, Lamb had noticed a distinct decline in the quality of the magazine, remarking 'The *London* I fear falls off.' Reminiscing nearly 20 years later, Hood wrote: 'How I used to look forward to Elia! And backward for Hazlitt, and all round for Edward Herbert, and how I used to *look up* to Allan Cunningham! for at that time the London had a goodly list of writers – a rare company.'[17]

Herbert was destined to play a vital part in Hood's development. His real name was John Hamilton Reynolds,[*] and the young Thomas Hood was frequently invited into the Reynolds household at Little Britain. As a close friend of Keats, he began to introduce Hood to a circle of new friends, particularly Lamb, who in turn introduced Hood to Wordsworth and Coleridge. By this time, however, Keats was no more than a memory to Mrs Reynolds and her disappointed daughters, for, after his unexpected engagement to Fanny Brawne and his final departure for Rome, they broke off with him. His death in 1821 ended their hopes of any rapprochement. Mrs Reynolds now had to look elsewhere for prospective husbands for her daughters. Judging from the tone of Hood's letters to one of the daughters, Marianne, we can assume that he was unusually fond of her ("…if you could imagine how very much I am pleased by whatever you say or do… I have a thousand reasons for loving you…."), but she rarely answered his letters and seems to have preferred another, for she married a Mr Green sometime before 1833. Hood's letters to another daughter, Charlotte, are full of paternal playfulness which did not anticipate any deeper attachment. It was to the quiet, more mature, charms of Jane that Hood turned. Eight years his senior, she was to stand by through the rigours of poverty and chronic ill-health in the years to come.

---

[*] John Hamilton Reynolds (1794-1852). Poet and satirist. Friend of Keats. Their correspondence is an important resource for Keats research. As brother-in-law to Thomas Hood, he played a significant part in Hood's early life. He was the son of George Reynolds, a teacher at Shrewsbury School, and Charlotte Jane Cox, a relation of the Hamilton family and therefore of William Hamilton Beckford, creator of the fantasy house, Fonthill, and author of oriental fantasy, *Vathek*.

As yet, in 1821, when Hood could hardly be described as healthy or wealthy, Mrs Reynolds was unimpressed. The important thing, however, was that Hood, through his friendship with John Hamilton Reynolds, had been introduced to the beauty of Keats' poetry, one of the most formative influences of his entire life. He dramatised Keats' *Lamia*. His poems, *The Plea of the Midsummer Fairies*, *Hero and Leander*, *Lycus the Centaur*, *Ode to Melancholy*, *Ruth*, and his sonnet *To Fancy*, all owe a considerable debt to the Keatsian idiom, though clearly Hood succeeds in imposing on his subject-matter his own brand of romantic feeling – more muted, more melancholy, more restrained – aspects that helped to make his poetry, and subsequently Keats', more popular with Victorian readers.

It may have been Reynolds who first introduced Hood to the art of punning, though Hood remarks circumspectly in the *Literary Reminiscences* that 'his jests, set off by a happy manner, are only ticklesome, but now and then they are sharp-flavoured, - like the sharpness of a pineapple'.

Although the *Literary Reminiscences* are fragmentary and incomplete ramblings, tinged with caricature, the fifth reminiscence has long been recognised as a valuable record of the Lamb circle and contains some of Hood's best prose. Lamb was 24 years older than Hood, yet there was a natural bond between them that paradoxically arose out of their differences. Whilst Hood had had a limited education, he was an avid reader, almost an auto-didact, full of fun, energetic, long-suffering in his better moments, whilst Lamb was more urbane, more refined, more erudite. Nevertheless, from today's perspective, we can only wonder at the breadth and variety of Hood's knowledge and learning.

He had met Lamb while working on the *London Magazine*, an event he recalls with great clarity:

> I was sitting one morning beside our Editor, busily correcting proofs, when a visitor was announced,…and in came a stranger – a figure remarkable at a glance, with a fine head on a small spare body, supported by two almost immaterial legs. He was clothed in sables of a by-gone fashion, but there was something wanting, or something present about him, that certified he was neither divine nor a physician, nor a school master: from a certain neatness and sobriety in his dress, coupled with his sedate bearing, he might have been taken, but that such a costume would be anomalous, for a Quaker in black. He looked still more like (what he really was) a literary Modern Antique, a New-Old Author... the delightful Essayist, the capital Critic, the pleasant Wit and Humourist, the delicate-minded and

large-hearted Charles Lamb! He was shy, like myself, with strangers, so that, despite my yearnings, our first meeting scarcely amounted to any introduction.[18]

Lamb, to whom he was to dedicate *The Plea of the Midsummer Fairies*, became one of Hood's closest friends. Through Lamb, Hood was able to extend his social circle at evening parties at Colebrooke Cottage, Lamb's home in Islington, 'where somebody who was somebody, or a literary friend, was sure to drop in.' On one occasion he met John Clare, of whom Hood wrote later:

> ....shining verdantly out of grave-coloured suits of the literati. In his bright, grass-coloured coat, and yellow waistcoat...he looks a very Cowslip, and blooms amongst us as Goldsmith must have done in his peach blossom... He was hardy, rough, and clumsy enough to look truly rustic....he was tender-hearted and averse to violence.[19]

Strolling home with Lamb after one of the literary dinners and wending their way through the Strand, it was, he says, little wonder that 'the Peasant and Elia, Sylvanus et Urban, linked comfortably together; there arose the frequent cry of "Look at Tom and Jerry – there goes Tom and Jerry!" ' There too was Cunningham, tall and physically powerful, with 'something of the true moody poetical weather observable in the barometer of his face, alternating from Variable to Showery, from Stormy to Set Fair'. De Quincey does not escape notice, with his 'speculation in the eyes, a curl of the lip, and a general character in the outline, that reminds one of some portraits of Voltaire. And a philosopher he is every inch. He looks, thinks, writes, talks, and walks, eats and drinks, and no doubt sleeps philosophically – i.e. deliberately'.

On a visit to the Lambs at Colebrooke Cottage, Hood met Samuel Taylor Coleridge, to whom he dedicated *Hero and Leander* ('Thou art my friend, and friendly to my rhyme.'), and vividly recorded his impressions:

> What a contrast to Lamb was the full-bodied Poet, with his waving white hair, and his face round, ruddy, and unfurrowed as a holy Friar's!...What a benign, smiling face it was! What a comfortable, respectable figure!...What a model....for a Christian bishop! But he was, perhaps, scarcely orthodox enough to be trusted with a mitre....For instance, he said, there are persons who place the whole angelical beatitude in the possession of a pair of wings to flap about with, like "a sort of celestial poultry". After

dinner he got up, and began pacing to and fro, with his hands behind his back, talking and walking, as Lamb laughingly hinted, as if qualifying for an itinerant preacher....With his fine flowing voice, it was glorious music, of the 'never-ending, still-beginning' kind; and you did not wish it to end......He had a spell in his voice that would not let you go. To attempt to describe my own feelings afterward, I had been carried, spiralling, up to heaven by a whirlwind intertwisted with sunbeams, giddy and dazzled, but not displeased, and had then been rained down again with a shower of mundane stocks and stones that battered out of me all recollection of what I had heard, and what I had seen.

If Keats was the most important formative influence on the development of Hood's romantic style, and Coleridge provided an effective stanza for his more dramatic or macabre productions, then Wordsworth must be given his rightful place as the poet who satisfied Hood's more tender aspirations, especially in his treatment of the 'common life', and domestic and familiar themes of sentiment and sorrow. Their meeting was arranged by his Islington friend and neighbour, Charles Lamb, who invited them both to tea at Colebrooke Cottage. Judging from the brevity with which Hood deals with the occasion in the fifth of his *Literary Reminiscences*, and the unexpected flippancy in the tone of his account of it, we can safely assume that the meeting was not particularly successful:

> In spite of any idle jests to the contrary, the name had a spell on it that drew me to Colebrooke Cottage with more alacrity than consisted with prudence, stiff joints, and a North wind. But I was willing to run, at least hobble, some risk, to be a party in a parlour with the author of Laodamia and Hartleap Well... If he has babbled, sometimes, like an infant of *two*-years old; he has also thought, and felt, and spoken, the beautiful fancies, and tender affections, and artless language, of the children who can say "We are *seven*". Along with the food for babes, he has furnished strong meat for men.
>
> So I put on my great-coat, and in a few minutes found myself, for the first time, at a door, that opened to me as frankly as its master's heart; for, without any preliminaries of hall, passage, or parlour, one single step across the threshold brought me into the sitting-room, and in sight of the domestic hearth. The room looked brown with "old

bokes", and beside the fire sate Wordsworth, and his sister, the hospitable Elia, and the excellent Bridget. As for the bard of Rydal, his outward man did not, perhaps, disappoint me; but the *palaver*, as the Indians say, fell short of my anticipation. Perhaps my memory is at fault; 'twas many years ago, and, unlike the biographer of Johnson, I have never made Bozziness my business. However, excepting a discussion on the value of promissory notes issued by our younger poets, wherein Wordsworth named Shelley, and Lamb took John Keats for choice, there was nothing of literary interest upon the carpet. But a book man cannot always be bookish. A poet, even a Rydal one, must be glad at times to descend from Saddleback, and feel his legs... It is a "Vulgar Error" to suppose that an author must be always authoring, even with his feet on the fender.[20]

Hood once mentioned these literary meetings to a gentleman of his acquaintance who, likening them to his parochial mutual instruction evenings, remarked: 'Yes, yes, all very proper and praiseworthy – of course, you go there *to improve your minds.*' There seems to have been little about Hood's meeting with Wordsworth that could be said to have in any way improved the mind. In a sonnet, written some years later, Hood bemoans the fact that, with Shelley (the lark) and Keats (the nightingale) dead, there is no poet alive to speak out as they had done. This was a mild reprimand to Wordsworth, who, on receiving a civil list pension in 1842, and the Poet-Laureateship in 1843, was seen to have recanted on his old radical ideas in favour of a more moderate politics. He was the 'The Lost Leader' who, in Hood's view, had failed to fill the poetical abyss caused by the deaths of the younger poets, Keats in 1821, and Shelley in 1822.

Despite this, Hood admired Wordsworth's poetry with its passionate evocations of nature. What Hood learned from Wordsworth was a skill in the composition of sweet and tender lyrics, the simple sentiments of which make little demand on the reader and are forgotten almost as soon as read.

The warm humanity of the *Literary Reminiscences* brings to life members of those literary meetings. The descriptions of Lamb and Coleridge are notable contributions to literary biography, revealing Hood as a quietly observant and meticulous writer of prose. They are sometimes fanciful, sometimes unreliable, but always revealing portraits that bring us closer to their subjects in a personal way.

44

TIME OF ROSES

It was not in the Winter
　Our loving lot was cast;
It was the time of roses—
　We pluck'd them as we pass'd!

That churlish season never frown'd
　On early lovers yet:
O no—the world was newly crown'd
　With flowers when first we met!

'Twas twilight, and I bade you go,
　But still you held me fast;
It was the time of roses—
　We pluck'd them as we pass'd!

Chapter 4 - Love and Marriage

At the age of 22, Hood moved into a life in which his talents could express themselves in many ways. The May 1822 issue of the *London Magazine* contained his ballad *Faithless Sally Brown* and the fragment *The Sea of Death*. In the same year, he collaborated with Reynolds in a dramatized version of *Gil Blas* by Le Sage, which was produced at the English Opera House in August 1822. Reynolds indeed was the most significant influence in Hood's life at this time. It is unlikely, however, that Hood met Keats, as there is no record of such a meeting before Hood joined the magazine and, by the time he had met Reynolds, Keats was already dead.

John Hamilton Reynolds spent his early working life in an insurance office and a solicitor's office, occupations which gave him little satisfaction since he spent much of his time reading English literature and the classics. He was largely self-educated, encouraged in this by a friend of his father's, John F. M. Dovaston, poet, naturalist and friend of the engraver, Thomas Bewick. Reynolds had, like Hood, a fanciful wit, and enjoyed playing practical jokes, which Hood readily agreed to join in with the rest of the family. He published several collections of poems, which received favourable reviews from Byron and Leigh Hunt. His friendship with Keats provided the romantic young Thomas Hood with the inspiration he most needed.[21]

For some unexplained reason, difficulties arose when, in the autumn of 1822, Hood announced his engagement to Reynolds's sister Jane. It appears that Mrs Reynolds had other plans for her daughter and opposed any idea of marriage to a poorly-paid sub-editor with pretensions of becoming a 'comic' poet! But Hood wrote to her, at the family home in Norfolk, a letter of such beauty and style that she was charmed and won over (at least temporarily) by her future son-in-law's devotion, thus expressed:

> My dear Mother,- - for so I may now call you, with how deep affection do I redeem all that I owe to that blessed name, feeling that I am indeed your son in perfect respect and duty. Only in this can I have deserved to be so dear to you, that you would bestow on me thus willingly an object of so much of your love as our excellent Jane. She is beside me while I pen this, and as I look at her, I know that what I write is a record of one eternal and unchangeable feeling which is to become more and more intense as I approach her great worth. So much the likeness of my wishes, − so

worthy of all admiration and affection that I should indeed exceed all others in the measure of my love as she in her virtues is excellent above all. Therefore I have singled her from the world, to be to me its grace and ornament, and its treasure above price, being proud above all things of her favour, and for this once, of my wisdom in this choice. And I desire that you should believe, that it is only for herself that I have loved, and will constantly while this life endures, which she has so blessed, and that in this only I can hold myself at all worthy of her invaluable heart. For I know that there is nothing like it in this world for excellence, and that its affection must of itself be my perfect happiness, whether I live or die, and in this knowledge I look forward with hopeful impatience to the time when I may claim her as mine forever.[22]

It is possible that Mrs Reynolds was not the first to be informed of the engagement and that she heard the news indirectly but, whatever the cause of her antagonism, Hood's impetuosity was forgiven, though possibly not forgotten, for his correspondence with Charles Wentworth Dilke reveals considerable tensions between Hood and the Reynolds family, ending in a mysterious estrangement between Jane and her brother. Nevertheless, further letters at this time of an intimate and friendly nature were written to Jane's younger sister Charlotte, showing Hood's spontaneous warmth and affection for the family into which he was to marry. His love of children put him on the very best of terms with them and even in small ways his sincerity and attractiveness are evident. There is, for example, a letter from Charlotte complaining that there is never any news in the country, to which Hood replied in his inimitable manner:

A barge must be an incident in your lives, − and a fired chimney like a comet in your Calendar. Pray, − last Sunday, exactly at 5p.m., did you observe a cloud – 52" 20° degrees North and very like a Whale. – It passed directly over my house and disappeared in the horizon. – You must have seen it for it was in broad daylight.[23]

The family must have loved him for his jokes and puns; his letters are rich with humorous description mingled with satire and sentiment. Sending a small present to Jane's baby niece, he writes: 'I feel much pleasure in sending her a little present, whilst she is so unconscious as she must be of the giver to show that my love is quite disinterested, and looks for no return'. In 1824, there is mention of an illness and of convalescing in the garden of their Queen Anne house in Islington.

In the summer he spent a brief holiday in Hastings, where he received a letter from Lamb giving advice on places to visit in the vicinity. He loved the sea and seized every opportunity of getting within reach of it. At Hastings, he enjoyed boating to his heart's content. On one occasion he nearly drowned; his boatman took the boat some way out from shore, Hood dived into the sea, but coming up for air he found himself under the boat. Diving again, he came up some distance from the boat, but having just recovered from a severe illness, he hardly had the strength to regain the boat. It proved a salutary warning to him ever after, as he would never bathe in the open sea again.[24]

In that year, Byron died. Hood's satirical work and odes, such as one addressed to Rae Wilson, show considerable affinities with the Byronic spirit but it was not until the early spring of 1825 that Hood began to make a name with the wider public. In collaboration with Reynolds, he published his *Odes and Addresses to Great People*, a collection of verse about celebrities of the period such as Sir Walter Scott ('The Great Unknown'), the prison-reformer Elizabeth Fry, George Colman (Licenser of Plays) and Joseph Grimaldi*, the clown. Lamb wrote a review of the work in the *New Times*, with a short dissertation on punning, which had been the basis of the satire. This punning was, in fact, so dexterous that, in spite of Gillman's suggestion that the *Odes* (published anonymously) might be by Reynolds and Hood, Coleridge believed them to be by Lamb himself.

Three months later, on 5 May 1825, Jane Reynolds and Thomas Hood were married at St Botolph's Church in Aldersgate and left for their honeymoon in Hastings. Five days passed before Jane wrote to her sister-in-law Elizabeth (Betsy) that, among other seaside pleasures, they had been invited aboard a man-of-war.

> I was whipped up in a chair, and we were conducted over the vessel by as handsome a young lieutenant as you could wish to see! It was unlucky I was married, as such an adventure to a single woman would have been advantageous......I am very much pleased with Hastings; we have had some beautiful walks, and have many more in store. I have not yet reached the Castle, nor Charles Lamb's little church, but the weather is very favourable to our little schemes, and we have no fault to find, but that a week has flown like a day, and we have only another to stay here.

* Joseph Grimaldi (1778-1837) was one of the greatest clowns in the history of English pantomime.

Your brother begs I will tell you that the town is empty, and that he is the handsomest man here! For this reason he drags me over the shingle every day, wearing out my shoes, that he may be seen! [25]

Hastings

In a letter to his new sisters-in-law from Hastings, Hood revealed in a very different tone his fury at the break-up of the *London Magazine* and vented his spleen on Hessey with a surprisingly vicious attack:

> 'In coming home I killed a viper in our serpentine path and Mrs. Fernor says I am by that token to overcome an enemy. Is it Taylor or Hessey dead? The reptile was dark and dull, his blood being yet sluggish from the cold; howbeit, he tried to bite, till I cut him in two with a stone. I thought of Hessey's long backbone as I did it. They are called adders – tell your father, because two & two of them together make four. Tomorrow we go to Lover's Seat [in Fairlight Glen], as it is called, to hallow it by our presence.'[26]

Admittedly, Hood felty badly let down in the last months of the *London Magazine*'s life, and was deeply disappointed at the break-up of his comfortable little literary world with the loss of a safe job with prospects. Hood was not the only one who suffered from hurt feelings, for we find

49

John Taylor, the magazine's editor, writing to Hessey in 1826: 'The loss of the London Magazine cut the string that tied us together, then I found that what was called Friendship was nothing but Self-Interest'.

In the following year, 1826, Hood published his first series of *Whims and Oddities in Prose and Verse*, illustrated with his own comic engravings. It was a collection of pieces he had written for the *London Magazine* and elsewhere, full of puns and verbal conceits in verse and prose, essays, stories and anecdotes, all with a serious vein of philosophising. In it were the poems *The Last Man, Faithless Sally Brown, A Winter Nosegay, Faithless Nelly Gray*, as well as some lesser-known poems. It was apparent from the book's success that the public wanted Hood to continue, as he put it 'to breathe his comic vein'. The punning continued in the second series of *Whims and Oddities*, which appeared in 1827 and contained such delights as Hood's satire on Thomas Moore's *The Wee Man*. From this time on, his prodigious talent for punning was to remain his hallmark. Public taste demanded it and few but Hood could provide the hungry reader with such tasty morsels.

> Oh Thomas Hood! Thou soul of fun,
> I know not one in London
> Better than thee to make a pun,
> Or better to be punn'd on!

Throughout these volumes there ran an undercurrent of sentiment as Hood searched for a stronger idiom - a more personal expression of the innermost thoughts and feelings of a sensitive poet whose public demanded not tears but laughter. In the same year Longmans published The *Plea of the Midsummer Fairies, Hero and Leander, Lycus the Centaur and other Poems*. It was his only collection of serious verse, containing a wealth of romantic yearning and self-communing, often rich in imagery and profoundly influenced by Keats, with stars shining more dimly from Shakespeare, Marlowe and Spenser. It includes some of Hood's best-known lyrics, including *Fair Ines, The Departure of Summer, Ode to Autumn*, the ballad *Spring it is Cheery*, together with *Ruth, The Sea of Death, I Remember,* and the sonnets *To Fancy* and *Silence*.

Hood's early poems are characterised by their youthfulness, abundance of fancy and preoccupation with fairies, centaurs and sea-nymphs. *The Plea of the Midsummer Fairies* is a long poem, as rich in colour and beneficent nature as *The Haunted House* was to be in gloom and malignant decay. In the poem Titania, Queen of the Fairies, whose kingdom is threatened by the jealous Time, begs Saturn (who represents the spirit of materialism) not to destroy the fairy world, which is the sweetness and beauty of life. It is an allegory of the struggle between pantheism and materialism; between the beauty of the soul of man and the cloak of civilisation that smothers it; and between the nobility of Natural Man and the impoverished spirit of the times - an allegory therefore of Rousseau's antithesis.

In it, the Queen speaks:

> O fret away the fabric of Fame,
> And grind down marble Caesars in the dust;
> Make tombs inscriptionless – raze each high name,
> And waste old armours of renown with rust:
> Do all of this, and thy revenge is just.

And Time replies:

> But would'st thou hear the melodies of Time,
> Listen when sleep and drowsy darkness roll
> Over hush'd cities, and the midnight chime
> Sounds from their hundred clocks, and deep bells toll
> Like the last knell over the dead world's soul.

In the poem, we move imperceptibly through a translucent world of green glades and crystal pools. When all seems lost and the destruction of the realm of fancy seems imminent, a stranger appears – a poet (Shakespeare) to whom the fairies turn and make their plea for immortality. The stranger listens as they cry in words worthy of Keats himself:

> O shield us then from this usurping Time,
> And we will visit thee in moonlight dreams;
> And teach thee tunes, to wed unto thy rhyme
> And dance about thee in all midnight gleams.

There is much of the spirit of *Endymion* in the poems, especially Hood's descriptions of nature, which is very similar to Keats's account of the after-life in the forest,[27] but Hood avoids Keats's dreaminess and writes in strong and impressive verse. It is clear from these few poems that Hood showed great promise as a serious poet and it was his greatest desire to be accepted as one by his public. Instead, the public registered its disapproval and, like Grimaldi's audience, called for 'a new feature'. Although at this time the romantic idiom came naturally to Hood, it was by no means an individual voice: his humorous nature led him to write in the comic manner, yet the opinion of several of his contemporaries, including Thackeray, Hartley Coleridge and Edgar Allan Poe, seems to be that Hood should have continued to write solely in the manner of his 1827 book, *Whims and Oddities*. After the publication of *The Plea of the Midsummer Fairies*, the

Monthly Review described him as a comic poet trying to play Hamlet. And he was driven back to whimsicality and punning humour, in which, it must be admitted, he had no peer in his own day.

> What is a modern poet's fate?
> To write his thoughts upon a slate; –
> The Critic spits on what is done, –
> Gives it a wipe, – and all is gone.[28]

If *The Plea of the Midsummer Fairies* and *To Fancy* were what Keats might have referred to as 'false beauty proceeding from art', then Hood did not find 'the true voice of feeling' until *The Song of the Shirt* and *The Haunted House*. At this period of his development, he was far more at home with wit and satire in the anti-romantic tradition of the later Byron but he vacillates between the two extremes. He cannot resist an occasional lyric or a sentimental verse or two. In the longer poems of the book, inspiration flags, as it does with many other poets of the time, but there is still much to admire. Of the shorter poems, *Fair Ines* is typical of his own romantic style, reminiscent of Moore and Burns and full of melancholy yearning. The sadness that comes with old age is the subject of *Ballad*:

> Spring it is cheery,
> Winter is dreary,
> Green leaves hang, but brown must fly;
> When he's forsaken,
> Wither'd and shaken,
> What can an old man do but die?

I Remember is perhaps the best known and has always been a favourite with anthologists from Palgrave to the present day. Its metrical weakness is entirely counter-balanced by its tender reminiscences and complete sincerity, so that the universal experience of childhood is enhanced and enlightened by the poetic truth of the imagery. If there is one quality that pervades all Hood's work, it is his deep understanding of man and nature, which at times exceeded his talent as a poet. But as Carlyle wrote in *Heroes and Hero-Worship*, 'It is a man's sincerity and depth of vision that makes him a great poet. See deep enough and you see musically; the heart of Nature being everywhere music; if you can only reach it'.

In his fairy world, Hood's creations do not have the humanity or warmth of Shakespeare's. They are not alive; he does not feel them enough to make them real; he does not love them enough to make them human. Yet his imagery is frequently subtle and always sensitive and beautiful. There is something of a rhapsody about this early poetry, with its dream-like ecstasy and romantic anguish. As Gilfillan says in his essay on Hood: 'His verse is not a chant but a carol. Deep as may be his internal melancholy, it expresses itself in and yields to song'.[29] Of the other longer poems, *Hero and Leander* and *The Two Swans* owe much to Marlowe and Spenser in poetic treatment but here again there is a Keatsian inflection to the language, in expressions such as 'serpent sorrow'. In style, *Lycus the Centaur* can be compared with Shelley's *Vision of the Sea* but the sensuality is once more Keatsian. These poems were in time eclipsed by the increasing popularity of the greater genius of Keats and early Tennyson, but it would be unfair to dismiss them as purely derivative. Referring to this volume, Edgar Allan Poe described Hood as 'one of the noblest, and, speaking of *Fancy*, one of the most singularly fanciful of modern poets'. Though *The Plea of the Midsummer Fairies and Other Poems* was a public failure, it was a private success. On the strength of this volume his more eminent contemporaries came to regard him as a man of genius. Mary Russell Mitford claimed him as the greatest poet of the 'Age of Transition', while Thackeray rated his serious poems among the best in English literature.

Meanwhile, Hood had given up engraving, though there is no doubt that his abilities in that field also lay in satire and caricature. He had in fact completed a plate for Neale's book on country houses published in the spring of 1821. It was a plate showing that he took this art seriously. In 1827 he produced engravings for Ackerman, including an illustration for Laurence Sterne's *Tristram Shandy**, depicting Corporal Trim demonstrating the ephemeral and uncertain nature of human life – a subject that fascinated Hood himself:

'Are we not here now? Continued the corporal (striking the end of his stick perpendicularly on the floor, so as to give an air of health and stability) – and are we not (dropping his hat upon the ground) gone in a moment!' It was this thought that inspired Hood to write his humorous monologue *Death in the Kitchen*.[30]

---

* *The Life and Opinions of Tristram Shandy, Gentleman*, novel by Laurence Sterne inspired by *Don Quixote*, published in nine volumes 1759-1767.

Chapter 5 - Punster and Caricaturist

As Hood's talents in poetry forced him into the pursuit of the comic, so his talent for drawing and sketching settled on the humorous forms of these arts and there arose a popular conception, which regrettably has superseded all others, that Hood's main intention was to make people laugh. His disregard for form and proportion, though it would have been disastrous in the work of a more serious artist, gave his drawings a strangely grotesque quality, almost a clumsiness, which accentuated the ungainly postures and movement of the human body. More broadly, it demonstrates how ineffectual we are in managing our own affairs and controlling our destiny. Hood did not stop there. He saw society with an eye for the weaknesses of human nature: the temptations, the silent whisperings of vice, the self-indulgence and the prejudice, pettiness, selfishness and hypocrisy of his age. As a caricaturist he sees all these traits, he exaggerates them and he blows them up into absurdities. But deep within the humour there is a kernel of despair that becomes increasingly apparent as we progress through the volume of his work.

In his engraving and sketching, his technical carelessness might suggest that he considered form as secondary, but this fault is mitigated by his ingenious draughtsmanship and subtle treatment of light and dark. As an engraver his technical resources were limited but he spent many hours at his workbench and produced many delightful and often transcendently humorous caricatures. These qualities, allied to his propensity for satire, are evident in the celebrated *Progress of Cant**, an elaborate cartoon which may have been designed as a frontispiece for the *Odes and Addresses to Great People*. Soon after its publication in 1825, Lamb wrote to a friend: 'We will get Hood, that half Hogarth, to meet you'. In his smaller works, Hood succeeds in combining his talents of drawing and verbal ingenuity in a satirical unity. The pictorial pun became an art form typical of his genius.

---

* *Progress of Cant* - see Part 2

AT THE TOP OF HIS PROFESSION

A-LAD-IN, or the wonderful LAMP

A BIRD IN THE HAND'S WORTH TWO IN THE BUSH

BEAUTIES OF SHAKSPEARE

Hood's Pen and ink cartoon sketches (this page and next three pages)

Dogmatical & Categorical –

DRAWING LOTS.

FLY-FISHING.

FRIENDS DROPPING IN.

First Fiddle

"Good Night! – Alls' Well!"

RUNNING SPIRITS

Following their honeymoon at Hastings, the Hoods returned to Islington in North London for a brief spell and then moved to 2 Robert Street, in the Adelphi, just off the Strand in central London. Hood's increasing popularity as a writer and reviewer led to an appointment as dramatic critic of a new Sunday newspaper, *The Atlas*. It seems that the Hoods had at last found true domestic happiness, for in their new home 'over against the Society of Arts' they became the centre of literary and theatrical gatherings of the kind that Mary Balmanno* describes in her memoir. One of the frequent visitors was the actress Fanny Kelly, to whom Hood records a debt of gratitude in the preface to the *Comic Annual* for 1834, where he says: 'I feel indebted to Miss Kelly for a copy of *Sally Simkin's Lament*, and still more so for the original of *Sally* herself, in the entertainment at the Strand Theatre; a personation of such admirable truth and nature, that even an incredulous public will be apt to take my Ballad Narratives for Facts not Fiction'.

The ballad was a form that Hood took to readily and developed in his own way, with the now famous Sally Simkin, Ben Bluff, Sally Brown, Ben the Carpenter, Lieutenant Luff and Faithless Nelly Gray as scapegoats for a sinister humour that found its roots in making laughter out of dramatic incidents in a manner very close to the spirit of melodrama. Some of his puns had macabre or gruesome anatomical details, as in *Mary's Ghost* and *Tim Turpin*. These poems of farce and grim circumstance are fused into a single Gothic absurdity, balanced by the versatility with which Hood imbues his characters and their sentiments. The ballad was a popular form and the public wanted comic situations in unusual settings. Hood provided them with ballads, most of which were set to music by Jonathan Blewitt and included in *The Ballad Singer*,[31] soon to be read in journals and comics and sung in theatres and music halls all over the country. The stories of the sailor who returns home to haunt his Sally after a shark has devoured his lower half, and of Ben the Carpenter who finds his Nelly has been unfaithful and has run off with another 'beau', captured the imagination of a new reading public. They were the fruit of Hood's predilection for the sinister and pathetic and were among the first examples of comic or sentimental Victorian ballads.

It was not long, however, before tragedy came to the house in Adelphi with the death, in May 1827, of Hood's first child, soon after it was born. 'In looking over some old papers,' Hood's son, Tom, wrote in *Memorials*, 'I found a few tiny curls of golden hair, as soft as the finest silk, wrapped in a yellow and time-worn paper inscribed in my father's handwriting:

---

* Mary Balmanno – English writer and artist born Mary Hudson in 1801, married Robert Balmanno in 1822 and emigrated with him to America around 1831. Died in Brooklyn, New York in 1875.

"Little eyes that scarce did see,
Little lips that never smiled;
Alas! my little dear dead child,
Death is thy father, and not me,
I but embraced thee, soon as he!" '[32]

Charles Lamb was moved to write a letter which, on first reading, would seem to be a breach of taste of the worst kind, but humour is often unintentionally cruel. 'Your news', he wrote, 'has spoil'd us a merry meeting. Miss Kelly and we were coming, but your letter elicited a flood of tears from Mary, and I saw she was not fit for a party. God bless you and the mother (or should-be mother) of your sweet girl that should have been. I have won a sexpence of Moxon by the sex of the dear gone one.' It was a poor pun for what was a tragic blow to the Hoods. In compensation, Jane received, soon after, a copy of Lamb's *On an Infant Dying as Soon as Born*.[33] Even in this delightfully sentimental piece Lamb could not resist an inevitable pun but this time it is done with affection rather than parched wit:

I saw where in the shroud did lurk
A curious frame of Nature's work,
A flow'ret crushed in the bud
A nameless piece of Babyhood.

In the summer, the Hoods saw less and less of the Lambs, who had moved to Enfield. At this time Hood was the object of invective in the *London Weekly Review*, whose literary critic, writing of a poem published in its rival the *Literary Gazette*, sneered: 'Mr. Hood bestows his tediousness on that most sage and chaste of periodicals'. It was not unusual for literary journals of the period to destroy reputations by invective, as we know from contemporary criticisms of Keats, Leigh Hunt and the rest of the 'Cockney school of poetry'. Hood seems to have realised the need to establish his position with the critics as well as the public and it is clear that, although he continued to supply his readers with comic material, his heart was still set on more serious compositions. In the preface to the *National Tales*[*] he remonstrates:

A life of mere laughter is like music without its bass; or a picture (conceive it) of vague unmitigated light; whereas the occasional melancholy, like those grand rich glooms of

_____

[*] *National Tales*. 2 vols. Ainsworth. 1827

old Rembrandt, produces an incomparable effect and a very grateful relief.

The *National Tales* were an attempt to overcome the prejudices of his readers, but failed. The style is flat and unconvincing. The plots are pale imitations of Boccaccio and writers of Gothic myth and legend. At times ingenious, they are all too often contrived, having none of the spontaneity of his early romantic Gothic poem, *The Bandit*. In spite of these shortcomings, *Blackwood's Magazine* praised some of the *Tales* as 'excellent, and few are without the impress of originality'.

In the closing months of 1827 Hood suffered a severe attack of rheumatic fever and was ordered to Brighton to convalesce. Sea air always benefitted his health, and he made regular visits to Brighton or his favourite seaside haunt, Hastings, for many years. Despite his ill health, he was full of spirit and hope, and enjoyed playing harmless practical jokes on his wife, who always took them in good humour. It was on their first visit to Brighton together that he tried to persuade Jane not to buy plaice with red spots because it was not fresh! So when the fishwoman came to the door Jane expressed doubt about the freshness of the fish, and was met with the assertion that they were not long out of the water, having been caught that morning. Gravely shaking her head, Jane observed, 'My good woman, it may be as you say, but I could not think of buying any plaice with those very unpleasant red spots!' The woman's answered with, 'Lord bless your eyes, Mum! Who ever see'd any without 'em?'[34]

At this time he became friendly with Robert Balmanno[*], secretary of the Artists' Benevolent Fund, Fellow of the Society of Arts, and a near neighbour of the Hoods in Adelphi. Jane and Thomas both wrote letters to the Balmannos from Brighton. In one such letter written in March 1828, Hood says how he walked about a mile on the shingles, partly against a strong wind, to his own and his wife's astonishment. 'We are now settled in a nice lively lodging – the sea frothing about twenty yards in front, and our side window looking down the road westward, and along the beach, where at about 100 yards lies the wreck of a poor sloop that came ashore the night we arrived – nobody lost.'[35] On their return, they visited the Lambs in their new home at Enfield in North London to eat a feast of bubble and squeak.

In 1828, the clown, Grimaldi, gave his farewell performance at the Drury Lane Theatre and Hood composed an address for the occasion. Grimaldi lived in Calshot Street in Islington, close to the Hood's old home. He performed for many years at Sadler's Wells and was one of the originators of English pantomime. Writing in the *London Gazette* just

---

[*] Husband of Mary Balmanno (see previous page)

before Grimaldi's retirement, Hood remarked with a note of wistfulness: 'After that night the red-and-white features of Joe Grimaldi will belong to tradition! Thenceforth he will be dead to his vocation, – but the pleasant recollections of his admirable fooling will still live with childhood, manhood, and with – T. Hood'.

Sheer Pretension !

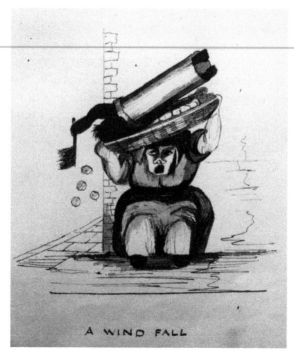

A WIND FALL

Kingsway, Brighton, by Thomas Hood

Royal Pavilion, Brighton by Thomas Hood (who called it 'Brazen Palace')

Chapter 6 - Phobias and Nightmares

In May 1828, Hood called on Sir Walter Scott, to whom he had dedicated the second series of *Whims and Oddities* (1827). The visit seems to have been a brief and informal one, since the 'Great Unknown' was finishing his *toilette* in order to dine at the Duchess of Kent's. Hood had ideas for a new annual to be supported by poems and essays from Lamb, Mary Russell Mitford, Hartley Coleridge, Keats, and Scott himself. *The Gem - A Literary Annual* was published in 1829 and was an astounding success, with all 5000 copies of the first edition sold. In spite of the glittering array of contributors, the undoubted masterpiece of the whole book was by Hood himself, his narrative poem *The Dream of Eugene Aram.*

The Dream is one of the most significant and remarkable poems in the history of Gothic literature. The contrast between the natural and the supernatural became the stock-in-trade of the Romantic idea of Gothicism. Like Horace Walpole's *The Castle of Otranto,* and Coleridge's *The Rime of the Ancient Mariner* and *Kubla Khan,* it was inspired by the nebulous world of dreams and nightmares and by the relationships between man and ectoplasm, between conscious and subconscious, and between daydreams and nightmares. These influences were soon to be extended to and associated with morbid psychological states, phobias and evil premonitions, battling with an ever-strengthening sense of sin. In his interesting and in some ways remarkable essay *Diabolical Suggestions*,[*] Hood had this to say on the origin of criminality:

> It is quite possible that the first fearful hint was the offspring of a dream – either a sleeping or waking one – for the opening of the outward organ does not simultaneously close that other eye, which gazes inwardly at another theatre, with its own stage, its own scenery, its own actors, and its own dramas. From the fragments of visionary tragedy, just abruptly terminated, it was quite possible for the imagination to compound a new plot, incoherently mixed up with the dawning actualities of the house and its inmates. And hence the catastrophe. The mere entrance and entertainment of an unlawful speculation in an ignorant, vicious, and ill-governed mind seems to involve the working out of the scheme. The more atrocious the proposal, the more vividly it presents itself, – the more horrible its features, the more frequently they recur; as a bad dream is oftener remembered than a good one. The man becomes in reality the slave to his own depraved imagination – its persecutions wear out what remains of his better nature, and submitting at last to its goadings, he performs the abominable task. Thus the Killing in Thought begets the Killing in Act; for which reason, perhaps, the first Murderer was branded, not in the hand, but on the forehead…An atrocious idea, wantonly entertained in the first instance, is pampered and indulged, till, like a spoilt child it tyrannises over its parent; and vociferously overwhelming the still small voice of conscience and reason – perhaps stiller and smaller than usual, in the individual – compels him to submit to the growing impetuousness of its dictates. The mind – the sober, honest, and industrious servant of the wise and good – is the lord and master of the weak and wicked. And this is especially true of the Imagination lovely and beneficent as the delicate Ariel under the command of a gifted Prospero – but headstrong, brutish, and devilish as Caliban turned out – according to a later history – when the wand that held him in subjection was broken!

[*] *New Monthly Magazine* 1842

Diabolical Suggestions was written in 1832, the year in which Bulwer-Lytton's novel *Eugene Aram* appeared. The novel is a sermon on the perils of yielding to evil thoughts or, as Hood put it, 'diabolical suggestions', which are the beginnings of crime and the nucleus of a greater evil. Deep within the human personality rests the origin of sin – man's eternal heritage, which if nourished by suggestion and circumstances grows into a monstrous serpent that eats away the veneer of upbringing and education and feeds on the contents of Pandora's Box. The seed of evil germinates and grows – unless Christianity destroys it. Lytton makes hardly any distinction between virtue and vice, seeming to condone rather than condemn the criminal, because of his belief in the concept of extenuating circumstances. The novel is pervaded by a sinister depravity. In Hood's poem, which appeared three years before Lytton's work, the conception is tenuous but strong, says Gilfillan. While Lytton's hero is 'a sublime demon in love', Hood's is 'a mere man in misery'. Hood singles out the moment when the dark recesses of the conscience are opened by the scalpel of remorse. The result is intense and horrible. In his treatment of the narrative, there are subtle interchanges between innocence and evil, purity and sin, inner peace and furtive fear, and conscience and peace of mind. In these nuances there is a Gothic intensity as overpowering as that of Hogg's *The Private Memoirs and Confessions of a Justified Sinner*, published in 1824.

We must remember too, we are not in London; we are in Northampton, a small, gossipy town with a deal of superstition and witchery about. Outside the provincial cities and towns of England, life was hazardous for travellers, who suffered not only the rigours of inclement weather, uncomfortable bone-shaking transport and, for riders, long hours, often days, in the saddle. Highwaymen lurked in deserted stretches of countryside, threatening terrified passengers at pistol-point and stealing their valuables, sometimes even the very clothes they stood up in, especially if they were of fine silks and embroideries.

In London, the combination of overcrowded dwelling-houses and abject poverty brought out resentments and even hatreds in the under-privileged part of the social order, an uneasy threat to the *status quo*. Honesty, decency and decorum were the province of the more affluent classes, though some well-known individuals sailed close to the wind and found themselves before the courts. The streets were so dangerous by the 1670s that James I was forced to bring in a Stabbing Act. Street crime throughout the 17th and 18th centuries was rife. Town-dwellers took their lives in their hands as they stepped from their front doors, almost immediately to be assailed by pickpockets, and beggars selling broadsides and tawdry trinkets. Children could be kidnapped, boys forced into nefarious activities, girls sold into the hardships of service and prostitution.

Violent times deserved violent punishments. Most criminals had a run of luck for a time but most traitors, murderers, highwaymen, cutters and maimers, forgers, housebreakers, rapists, and rustlers ended up on the gallows, a fearsome end also for housebreakers, stealers of letters, common burglars – that is, all those who had the misfortune to be caught. Some more successful rogues, sporting their stolen finery, were bold enough to appear in the salons and drawing-rooms of the rich and powerful, but more often than not they made a fatal slip and, after a summary trial, spent their last night in Newgate Prison before making their journey to a public place of execution. During Hood's lifetime, there were no less than 65 public hangings, including the wily highwayman, Galloping Dick (1800); the murderers, John Holloway and Owen Haggarty (1807), at whose execution 28 spectators were trodden to death; John Bellingham, the murderer of the Prime Minister, Spencer Perceval; the poisoner, Ellen Fenning (1815, believed to be innocent); the ruthless Cato Street Gang (1820); the banker and forger, Henry Fauntleroy (1824); the *faux* coiner, Edward Lowe (1827); William Corder, murderer of Maria Marten (1828), and François Benjamin Courvoisier, murderer of Lord William Russell (1840), among many other sensational cases. Public executions were a spectator sport; Dickens attended one attracting 30,000 people, hiring a special place for himself with a clear view of the gallows. Thomas Hardy saw his first execution at the age of 16, perched in a tree to get a good view. We have to excuse their interest, considering the social mores of the time which accepted the inevitable, and, after all, they were authors in search of material.

This voyeuristic, sadistic side of Hood's writings is of fascinating aspect, and appears in a number of guises, both comic and serious throughout his work. His brain pullulated with a myriad images of death and mutilation, complemented by an equally rich cluster of images celebrating the fullness of life. In his early work, there is a striving to identify himself with the beautiful, the world of nature, myth and legend, bolstered by a wide spectrum of natural imagery. But his more mature writings show a darker side, a coming to terms with the reality of existence. Perhaps God is not, after all, in his Heaven, as Browning hopes, and all is not right with the world. The human psyche is governed not by fairies but phantoms. This sombre view is expressed in Aram's confession, balanced by the sweet innocence of the young boy, who will never be quite the same again, tainted as he is by the presence of evil, which has entered the very centre of his being. In Blake's words:

> Oh, Rose, thou art sick!
> The invisible worm,
> That flies in the night,
> In the howling storm,

Has found out thy bed
Of crimson joy;
And his dark secret love
Does thy life destroy.

The Dream of Eugene Aram was the first poem to bring Hood fame in the wider world of sophisticated readers. In it, he displayed a subtle psychological insight into the treatment of sinister themes. The unreal past looms like a hideous phantom as the stark horror and self- torture raging in the soul of the usher in the poem is revealed against the innocence of the child, as he listens to the confession and learns the truth. There is something of the grimness of Hood's ballads here, but shorn of punning.

The poem is a powerful example of Hood's skill in writing narrative verse, and its impact on the reading public was phenomenal. Aram, while working as a schoolmaster in Knaresborough, was suspected of murdering a shoemaker, Daniel Clark, in 1744 for his jewellery and silver. Some years later, when Aram had moved to King's Lynn, a skeleton was dug up in Knaresborough, and suspicion again fell on Aram who had confessed that he knew where Clark was buried. Aram was arrested and, in a sensational trial, made an eloquent though unsuccessful defence, He was hanged in 1759. Hood takes the moment when the murderer, in an effort to relieve his tormented soul, confesses his crime to an innocent child in his care:

'All night I lay in agony,
In anguish dark and deep;
My fever'd eyes I dared not close,
But stared aghast at Sleep:
For Sin had render'd unto her
The keys of Hell to keep!

'All night I lay in agony,
From weary chime to chime,
With one besetting horrid hint,
That rack'd me all the time, -
A mighty yearning, like the first
Fierce impulse into crime!

'One stern tyrannic thought, that made
All other thoughts its slave;
Stronger and stronger every pulse
Did that temptation crave, -
Still urging me to go and see
The Dead Man in his grave!

The cumulative effect of the stanzas gives a sustained sense of doom to the work. It is a masterpiece of its genre. Its success was immediate, and Hood reissued it separately in 1831, with illustrations by William Harvey.

Sir John Bowring, a contributor to *The Gem*, noted: 'I have read that *Aram* story, which I will put by the side of the very grandest productions of poetical conception'. To Bernard Barton he wrote:

> What fertile genius (and a quiet good soul withal) is Hood. He has 50 things in hand, farces to supply the Adelphi Theatre for the season, a comedy for one of the great theatres, just ready, a whole entertainment by himself for Matthews and Yates to figure in, a meditated Comic Annual for the next year, to be nearly done by himself. You'd like him very much.

In spite of the success of *The Gem*, all was not well between Hood and his publisher, William Marshall. It appeared that Marshall was withholding payments due to Hood, and the latter pulled out, only editing the first of four annual issues. He had had enough of Marshall's business methods. A letter written by Hartley Coleridge to his mother about the matter in 1829 is illuminating:

> …I have received a letter from Mr Hood's brother [i.e., brother-in-law, John Hamilton Reynolds] informing me that Mr Hood has declined the Editorship of that work – referring me for payment to Mr Marshall – N, –1 Holborn Bars, the person whose name I was applied to for contributions to The Gem, with the somewhat unacceptable information that said Mr Marshall is a very mean, impracticable, disagreeable sort of personage… Hood is going to publish a comic Annual. I wish his speculation may not prove a tragedy to himself and a farce to the rest of the world. He is a man of real genius, and I wish him well.

It was not the first, and it would not be the last, time that Hood fell out with his publishers. But this is not to suggest that Hood's experience of the ways of publishers was all acrimony and hypocrisy. Being the gentle, amiable man that he was, he had no difficulty making friends, even among publishers and editors. Many of his letters to publishers betray a warmth of friendship that surmounted the perils and dangers of outrageous publishers' fortunes (or even publishers' outrageous fortunes, for that matter). But some of his relationships are a sorry tale of deceit and underhandedness, and he was faced with a desperate necessity of maintaining a regular income through his own industry and ingenuity. Hood typifies Isaac D'Israeli's description of the impoverished author:

> Authors continue poor, and booksellers become opulent, an extraordinary result! Booksellers are not agents for authors, but the proprietors of their works; so that the perpetual revenues of literature are solely in possession of the trade. Is it then wonderful that even successful authors are indigent? They are heirs to fortunes, but, by a strange singularity, they are disinherited at birth.[36]

Chapter 7 - Parody and Punning

Hood now moved into a happier period of his life, enjoying the company of many new friends and ever-increasing popularity and success. Possibly with a view to being closer to the Lambs or because he wanted a more rural setting and healthy country air, in 1829 he moved to the London suburb of Enfield, where he and Jane found a delightful house at Winchmore Hill called 'Rose Cottage', with a sheltered garden full of trees and shrubs.

Rose Cottage, Winchmore Hill (from *Memorials*, p53)

An amusing incident took place during the move. A large hamper of china and glass arrived one morning, and its contents were temporarily placed on a newly-erected wooden shelf. Of course, the shelf fell down with all the weight on it, whereupon Hood calmly surveyed the damage, remarking 'the china which *came up* in the morning, had *come down* in the evening!'[37]

In the same year that *The Dream of Eugene Aram* appeared, Hood published his long ballad *The Epping Hunt* – a poem abundant with puns.

As we have seen, Lamb too was not averse to making puns on the names of his friends as Hood does here in this example:

> And some had horses of their own,
> And some were forced to job it;
> And some while they inclined to *Hunt*,[*]
> Betook themselves to *Cob-it* [†]

Perhaps no author in the whole of English literature has been at once so admired and detested as Hood for his verbal conceits and overtones of wit. The 18th century defence of the pun rested on Swift's aphorism: 'None despise puns but those who cannot make them'. Dr Johnson deftly refuted this with: 'He who would make a pun would pick a pocket' – a remark that prompted Hood to write a tart parody of the great doctor's style in 'Johnsoniana', written in the form of a letter to the editor of the *Comic Annual* (i.e. Hood himself), ending: 'Apologistically requesting indulgence for the epistolary laxity of an unpremeditated effusion'. The pun, for Hood, was no unpremeditated effusion. It was a literary conceit to be respected and meticulously worked at, though not laboured. He was not attempting to 'falsify the brain with juggling mockeries', as Apollonius says in *Lamia* (Hood's version, not Keats's). Typical of Hood's style of punning are these three verses from the ballad *Lieutenant Luff* in which the puns are increasingly adventurous and adroit:

> A sober man he might have been,
> Except in one regard,
> He did not like *soft* water,
> So he took to *drinking hard*!
>
> According to this kind of taste
> Did he indulge his drouth,
> And being fond of *Port*, he made
> A *port-* hole of his mouth!
>
> Full soon the sad effects of this
> His frame began to show,
> For that old enemy the gout
> Had taken him in *toe*!

---

[*] John Hunt, one of Byron's publishers, and brother of Leigh Hunt
[†] William Cobbett

Perhaps the most celebrated of all are the last two lines of *Faithless Sally Brown*[38]:

> They went and told the sexton, and
> The sexton toll'd the bell.

At first Hood adopted the practice of printing the puns in italics, a practice that he later dropped as the result of certain criticisms. While some critics objected to the way in which they were printed, others felt a strong antipathy towards punning as a literary conceit. In the preface to the *Comic Annual* for 1834, Hood was compelled to justify himself to an ever-increasing readership in these words: 'It will of course be objected as heretofore, by certain reviewers, that my pages swarm with puns; but having taken out a certificate to 'shoot folly as it flies,' I shall persist in using the double barrel as long as meanings will rise in coveys.' In the second edition of *Whims and Oddities,* he displayed some irritation towards his antagonists, saying: 'I am informed that certain monthly, weekly, and everyday critics, have taken great offence at my puns: and I conceive how some Gentlemen with one idea must be perplexed by a double meaning'.

There were some admirers among his circle of friends – particularly Cunningham – who, on receiving a copy of the first series of *Whims and Oddities*, scribbled off a note to Hood: 'There was enough of wit visible at first reading to ensure a second, and at a second so many new points appeared that I ventured on a third, and with the fourth I suppose I shall go on discovering and laughing....I believe a smile carries a higher market price than a sigh, and that a laugh brings more money than deeper emotion'. In the second series, Hood is rather more apologetic, referring to his 'verbal misdemeanors' for which he is 'once more guilty' and 'for which, I must leave my defence to Dean Swift, and other European and Oriental Pundits. Let me suggest, however, that the pun is somewhat like a cherry: though there may be a slight outward indication of partition – of duplicity of meaning – yet no gentleman need make two bites at it against his own pleasure'.

Hood's punning was the product of a transcendent talent for seeing analogies and associations where others saw only single meanings. His lively and alert mind forced him to see life in terms of 'duplicities'. He was largely responsible for the restoration of the pun, which had fallen into disrepute after the Elizabethan period, and by keeping it alive was merely expressing the idiom of people heard in taverns and music halls – an idiom that triumphed in the hands of Shakespeare and James Joyce. Words as well as thoughts and actions exist in sensitive minds more by association than by singularity but there are times when we feel that, in the case of Hood, the pun is a kind of verbal self-abuse that becomes so much a part of his being that he cannot resist it even when the pun is bad. So the habit becomes a disease. His inner eye sees minute and delicate resemblances in sounds and sights, which – when translated into words – reveal the complexities of his thought processes. His versatile and prolific mind produced a wide range of poems, essays, reviews, stories, letters and prefaces enormously rich in double meanings. Lamb, when commenting on the *Odes and Addresses*, foresaw its dangers, saying: 'A pun is good when it can rely on single self; but called in as an accessory, it weakens, – unless it makes humour, it enfeebles it.' This is not entirely true, for the delight of the pun about Lieutenant Luff's gout cannot be bettered. Nevertheless, the subtle kind of punning that Lamb was thinking of may be seen in this verse from *The Epping Hunt*[39]:

> So off they scampered, man and horse,
> As time and temper pressed –
> But Huggins, hitching on a tree,
> *Branched* off from all the rest.

Hood possessed innate egocentricity – a state not so far from eccentricity. In habits and mannerisms he was by no means extrovert, yet his mind and imagination were ever active and his quiet humour was as much a part of his nature as his curious whimsy and riotous practical-joking. His wit was the expression of a lively and intelligent mind contained in a frail and sick body. It was the natural effusion of his love of life and people. It was not (and is not) acceptable to all, for to read Hood and enjoy him it is necessary to be versatile: to enter into the spirit of the clowning, which is to be a quick-change artist with a new mask (perhaps a sad one), to make people laugh and to jump through grammar like a circus dog through a hoop. He can be scathing, sentimental, humorous, lyrical, pathetic, dry-humoured or tear-drenched. We can feel so many emotions at once that we lose sight of the poet as he slips into the maze of his 'Grotesques and Arabesques and droll Picturesques', and dances in and out of the turmoil of farce, hilarity, mystery and pathos. Hood's very reputation depended on his puns and his jokes. Because of this, few were prepared to accept him as a serious poet, even after *The Dream of Eugene Aram*. When John Hamilton Reynolds met Fanny Brawne at a ball, their conversation ran thus:

Reynolds: (admiring Fanny's dress which was decorated with bugles). It's good to wear bugles and be heard wherever one goes.
Fanny: *And it's good to be a brother-in-law of Tom Hood's and get jokes for nothing.*

The matter of Hood's puns was finally settled by G.K. Chesterton in his account of Victorian Literature:

> In the long great roll that includes Homer and Shakespeare, he was the last great man who really employed the pun. His puns were not all good (nor were Shakespeare's), but the least of them were a strong and fresh form of art. The pun is said to be a thing of two meanings; but with Hood there were three meanings, for there was also the abstract truth that would have been there with no pun at all.[40]

Too cold to Bear !

Emigration : meeting a settler !

Chapter 8 - The Comic Annuals

Another of Hood's business ventures was part-ownership of the literary magazine *The Athenaeum*, together with John Hamilton Reynolds, Allan Cunningham and Charles Wentworth Dilke, the last of whom was to support Hood in a time of ill health and financial difficulty. Founded in 1828 by James Silk Buckingham, it had failed to become profitable, and by 1830 Dilke had become its sole editor. To Hood's dismay, in 1831 he made the surprising decision to halve the price of the paper. For Hood, this was a reckless act, reducing the profits and his own meagre income, and he withdrew from the paper, together with his brother-in-law, John Hamilton Reynolds. Despite this, Dilke was determined to carry his policy through to the bitter end, except that, as it happened, the end was not bitter but sweet, for the paper's sales went up by six times the former circulation. The financial future of *The Athenaeum* was assured, which could not be said for Hood's. A degree of affluence had been within his grasp, and he had refused to take the risk. However, the literary and critical support the paper was to give him in future would be of invaluable assistance, and Hood continued as a regular contributor for the rest of his life, his most important contributions being those on copyright, published in 1837.

In 1829 Hood started work on his famous *Comic Annuals*. The first issue appeared in 1830, and was dedicated to Sir Francis Freeling, the Postmaster General, in his capacity as 'the great Patron of Letters'. But with the addition of some fifty of Hood's humorous wood-engravings, the printing of the first *Comic Annual* was fraught with problems. Hood, a perfectionist regarding the quality of printing and binding, was dismayed with the poor quality of the printing of the woodcuts, and a great deal of reprinting had to be done. In spite of the delays, which caused Hood considerable financial problems, the first edition was an unqualified critical success. The little gilt-edged volumes, with their plum-coloured spines and gilt lettering, their clever display of prosaic and poetical pleasures, interspersed with humorous wood-engravings, had a unique charm which was the delight of every reader from low-brow to high-brow.

The *Comic Annuals* played an important part in the early Victorian Christmas and were followed by many similar rival publications. Hood had in the past dedicated his work to those contemporaries that he most admired, such as Lamb, Coleridge and Scott. Now he turned to more eminent people such as Sir Francis Freeling, Viscountess Granville, the Duke of Devonshire (later to become his patron) and William IV.

On 11 September 1830, a daughter was born at Rose Cottage to Thomas and Jane Hood. Such was Hood's admiration for Sir Francis Freeling, they named her Frances Freeling after him. She would be known in the family as 'Fanny'. She married Rev. John Somerville Broderip at the age of 19, and went on to have a notable literary career herself.

A copy of the first volume of the *Comic Annuals* was sent as a present to the Duke of Devonshire. Before long, Hood received a commission from the Duke for a list of punning titles for sham books to be attached to a door leading to one of the gallery staircases to his library at Chatsworth. Hood obliged with a long list, including 'Lamb on the Death of Wolfe', 'A Chronological Account of the Date Tree', 'Boyle on Steam' and 'Johnson's Contradictionary'. It was to the Duke that the 1831 *Comic Annual* was dedicated, in recognition of his patronage of the Arts: "To His Grace The Duke of Devonshire, The Great Comptroller of All Public Performers, Kindly Countenancing Plays upon Words, as well as Plays upon Boards…"

Hood dedicated the *Comic Annual* for 1832 to William IV, "a Monarch so truly anxious to promote the happiness of his subjects", who was staying at the Royal Pavilion in Brighton. The King expressed a wish to meet his ambitious young poet and Hood duly set out on an arduous journey from London of some seven hours and, on arrival, according to his son, Tom, was received in audience in a 'cordial and hearty manner'. All went well until, on retiring, he backed out of the royal presence and forgot where the door was, but 'the King good humouredly laughed, and himself showed him the right direction, going with him to the door'.[41]

 Once more the Hood family made a move in 1832 – this time to Essex, to the former hunting lodge of Wanstead House, once the residence of the exiled Louis XVIII of France. The lodge, known as Lake House, faced south and commanded fine views across the Thames to Shooter's Hill. The rooms were adorned with murals in the French style. There was a fine 18th-century portico with sycamores on each side and a garden of shrubs, holly and rhododendron, through which one approached extensive grounds, on the edge of which was a gypsy encampment.

In spite of frequent attacks of rheumatic fever, Hood continued his practical joking, undaunted by external difficulties. Painting his daughter Fanny's favourite doll with bright pink spots one night, when she saw it the following morning she was convinced it had caught the measles, and dared not go near the doll. On another occasion, a friend pushed Hood into the lake at Wanstead. Hood pretended to drown by sinking below the surface and holding his breath. The friend, shocked and in great agitation, rushed back to the house for help. Jane and the children, dismayed at the prospect of imminent paternal deprivation, hastened to the lakeside to see what they could do to save Hood, but all they saw were ripples on the surface of the water. This sorry sight of horror-stricken faces was watched with glee by Hood, who was hiding behind a tree, drenched to the skin, and barely able to contain his amusement.

HOOD'S RESIDENCE AT WANSTEAD.

Lake House, Wanstead (from *Memorials*, p61, colourised version)

His health began to deteriorate and visits to the seaside resorts of Brighton and Ramsgate became urgent. A letter written in 1833 from Ramsgate is full of joking humour, including the following playful lines:

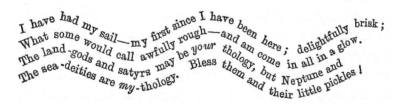

I have had my sail—my first since I have been here; delightfully brisk;
What some would call awfully rough—and am come in all in a glow.
The land-gods and satyrs may be your thology, but Neptune and
The sea-deities are my-thology. Bless them and their little pickles!

The clown was now beginning to drop his comic mask and put on his pathetic one, though he sometimes wore them both at once. He continued to work and planned a novel entitled *Tylney Hall* – a title derived from a former owner of Wanstead House, Earl Tylney. Hood felt that he could not be respectful enough to write sustained love scenes and was not satisfied with some of the characterisation. This element of love in human relationships was beyond his scope as a comic writer, though he had dealt with it successfully in some of his early lyrics. He always treated emotional issues with humour, so serious love-making did not find a happy place among his puns. Lamb referred to the novel as 'a medley; without confusion, of farce, melodrama, pantomime, comedy, tragedy, puncher'. Dickens wrote of it some years later:

> 'I have been reading poor Hood's *Tylney Hall*: the most extraordinary jumble of impossible extravagances, and especial cleverness I ever saw. The man drawn to the life from the private bookseller is wonderfully good; and his recommendation to a reduced gentleman from the university, to rise from nothing, as he the pirate did, and go round to the churches and see whether there's an opening, and begin by being a beadle, is one of the finest things I ever read, in its way.'

Tylney Hall was published in 1834, the year in which Hood became involved in business deals of a very unsatisfactory nature. With few copyright laws to speak of in his day, he was exploited by unscrupulous publishers, sending him crashing into bankruptcy – a blow from which he never fully recovered. Together with this came the death of a man to whom he had been devoted for many years – his 'literary father' Charles Lamb. This loss temporarily immobilised Hood physically and creatively. His generosity in entertaining his friends in grand style, in the extravagant surroundings of Lake House, in Wanstead hastened his financial collapse.

It must be said that he played the host in a most engaging and delightful manner that endeared him to all who had the opportunity of an invitation. But this generosity was a bone of contention with the Reynolds family, that he chose to live always beyond his means without the necessary financial security to back it. Charles MacFarlane, in his *Reminiscences of a Literary Life* gives a highly-coloured account of Hood's life at Winchmore Hill, and his subsequent removal to Lake House:

> Hood had no head for business, no system, no management, and he spent money as fast as he got it. For some time he occupied a pleasant little cottage in the right pleasant valley of Winchmore Hill... It was certainly house enough for him; but Tommy did not think so, and all of a sudden he was invaded by the insane fancy that he could save expenses and even make money by farming – he who scarcely knew grass-seed from gunpowder. So after a lucky hit with some book or other, he went away and took a large house on the edge of Epping Forest, quite a mansion and

79

manor-house, with extensive gardens and about eighty acres of land attached. As the house was so roomy, he could give his friends beds, and as a general rule those who went to dine stayed all night, and a part of the next day.

The house was seldom devoid of guests, the distance was so convenient, and Tommy's cockney friends liked to breathe the country air, and took up quite a romantic passion for the Forest. His household expenses were treble what they had been in the snug, pretty little cottage at Winchmore Hill: and then the farm ran away with a world of money. It may be imagined how a thorough cockney, one born and bred in the Poultry, Cheapside, a poet and punster, would farm! What with his hospitalities and what with his agricultural expenditure, he became seriously embarrassed.[42]

Such a description has something of the comical about it, yet we cannot deny that Hood's intentions were largely praiseworthy ones. His natural kindness and generosity, for example, was not as misdirected as MacFarlane suggests, yet there is some element of truth in the suggestion that Hood's tendency towards a certain 'grandiose folly' at this time had brought him to the point of bankruptcy. Such a prospect is horrendous at any time, but in Hood's day especially so. In the eighteen months following December 1825, no less than 101,000 writs of arrest were issued for debts unpaid. In the year ending 1830, 7114 persons were sent to the Debtors' Prison, in London alone. Hood could not, alas, benefit from the favourable and more humane changes that would come only a few years hence. Ironically, his new publisher, Alfred Head Baily[*], with whom he was to suffer considerable deceit, announced for publication *Scenes and Stories by a Clergyman in Debt*. This purported to have been written during the said clergyman's confinement in the Debtors' Prison, with factual accounts of usurers, sheriff's officers, attorneys, money-lenders 'and their tribe', and giving instances of the incarceration of the distressed tradesmen, fallen roués, practised swindlers, shipwrecked dramatists and, need it be mentioned, poor authors. *The Literary Gazette* reviewed it:

> The avowed object of this work is to demonstrate the evil
> of imprisonment for debt; and it is evidently the production
> of one who has tasted the bitterness of that condition, and

---

[*] Alfred Head Baily (1808-1884), printer and publisher. He published *Tylney Hall*, the *Comic Annuals* from 1835 to 1839, *Hood's Own* (1839) and eventually *Up the Rhine* (1840).

seen how ruinously the practice wrought both for the honest debtor and merciless creditor. The *subject* is one of great national interest, and as far as this exposition goes, we trust it will increase the attention which humanity and policy have already directed to the application of a remedy.

This review is testimony of the horrors that awaited the bankrupt before legislation was introduced to protect the debtor from such indignities. If only Hood had read the book, perhaps he might just have been deterred from his reckless extravagance. Yet one doubts it, for his natural gregariousness and open-hearted friendship would not allow any such constraint. He succumbed with as much dignity as he could muster. After the final collapse of his interests, he wrote to Dilke 'the struggle to maintain caste is indeed a bitter one and after all I fear we must say, "le jeu ne vaut pas la chandelle" '.[43]

The fateful year of 1835 began auspiciously enough with the birth of a son on 19th January at Wanstead to Thomas and Jane, christened Tom. But before the year was out, Hood was to experience a flurry of misfortunes that would all but crush his spirit. It was to be the worst year of his life, when he was forced by the most distressing of circumstances to face up to the hardest and cruellest realities. First, the difficult birth of Tom Hood brought Jane to the very edge of death. For weeks she lay gravely ill at Lake House, Hood often sitting up all night with her and holding her hand to comfort her. The Reynolds sisters, Marianne and Charlotte, arrived from Norfolk to find the family living in conditions nothing short of poverty. They berated Hood for allowing their beloved sister, and her new-born child, to suffer such degradation, and threatened to remove them to more salubrious surroundings until such time as Hood could afford to keep them in some degree of comfort. Hood resisted these entreaties and threats, believing all the time that things would improve. Fortunately, Fanny caught the measles and the intransigent in-laws were driven from the house, leaving Hood to face an absolutely desperate financial crisis. He has no-one to turn to.

It seems that he was involved in some way with Branston and Wright, a contract perhaps, or a mutual commitment of some kind, and when the firm went bankrupt in 1833, Hood clearly found it difficult to meet the financial demands made on his meagre resources. Unlike many of the other business associations Hood formed in his life, he did not break off his friendship with Branston and Wright, and he seems to have been a loyal support to them in their time of crisis. In fact, he went so far as to allow Branston to set up a work-room over the stable at Lake House, and after Hood left the house, Branston moved in, to be the last tenant of the house before its demolition.

Threatened with complete destitution and mounting debts, in spite of a loan from the Duke of Devonshire the previous year, Hood was also battling all the time with a serious consumptive condition. When attacks of fever grew worse, he was forced to work from his bed, suffering alarming attacks of breathlessness and blood-spitting. He now faced the worst decision of his entire life: to stay and endure the suffering, shame and privation of the Debtors' Prison, or go into self-imposed exile.

Chapter 9 - Exile

To his credit, rather than face the degradation of the debtors' prison, Hood courageously decided that his only honourable course was to leave England, but not without the most agonising heartache. He had, in his life, made the closest of friendships, and now, two friends came forward to manage his affairs in his long absence abroad – Charles Wentworth Dilke and John Wright. Leaving his affairs in their capable hands, he bade an emotional farewell to his wife and children, whom he had placed in the care of Dr William Elliott (who had attended Jane during her long illness at Lake House). As Tom Hood recorded in the *Memorials* (1869), 'he voluntarily expatriated himself 'and, with sufficient money from an advance on future work in his pocket, boarded the steamship *Lord Melville,* bound for Rotterdam, in March 1835.

Some years before, in *The Plea of the Midsummer Fairies*, Hood had written a poem entitled 'The Exile'; he could not have realised how much meaning his youthful words would have in the future, still less that they should ever apply to himself:

> The swallow with summer
>   Will wing o'er the seas,
> The wind that I sigh to
>   Will visit thy trees,
> The ship that it hastens
>   Thy ports will contain,
> But me – I must never
>   See England again!
>
> There's many that weep there
>   But one weeps alone,
> For the tears that are falling
>   So far from her own;
> So far from thy own, love,
>   We know not our pain;
> If death is between us,
>   Or only the main.
>
> When the white cloud reclines
>   On the verge of the sea,
> I fancy the white cliffs,
>   And dream upon thee;

But the cloud spreads its wings
  To the blue heav'n and flies,
We never shall meet, love,
  Except in the skies!

Thus one chapter in the life of Thomas Hood was ended; the next was to be equally fraught with problems.

It was cruel trick of fate that the Copyright laws, the campaign for which Hood wholeheartedly supported in company with Charles Dickens and Thomas Carlyle, came too late to save him from the dark threat of bankruptcy. He was by no means alone. The streets of Paris and Ostend were crowded with British exiles, debtors mercilessly driven from their homeland, some unlikely to return for many years for fear of imprisonment, possibly for life, if they failed to satisfy their creditors. Hood brought to mind Defoe's financial failure in 1692, which ended in his being 'honourably discharged in full debts'. Hood wrote in December 1835 that 'The example of Defoe is ever before me.'[44] The key for Hood was honesty, to be 'honourably discharged' in all things, and he faced his grim future with all the courage he could muster, supported by his devoted, ever-reliable wife Jane.

On the journey he suffered terribly from a great storm off the coast of Holland; the steamship was buffeted by gigantic waves, its passengers and crew believing their very lives to be in danger. The severity of the storm brought disaster to eleven other ships along the Dutch coast. The captain and three of his crew were almost pitched into the sea. It affected him irreparably, seeming to activate the physical weakness of his body into a raging sickness that ceased only with his death ten years later. In his letters to Jane, these experiences are veiled and blurred by a touching humour, in an effort to conceal his true state of health. He wrote to Jane from Coblenz:

> 'I was *sea-sick* and *frightened* at sea for the first time: so you will suppose it was no trifle: in fact it was unusually severe. I went up at midnight and found *four* men at the helm, hint enough for me, so I went down again, and in the morning a terrific sea tore the whole four from the helm, threw the captain as far as the funnel (twenty paces) and the three men after him. Had it not come *direct aft*, it would have swept them into the sea, boat, skylights, and everything in short, and have left us a complete wreck... But it made me very ill, for it was like being shaken up in a dice box, and I have had a sort of bilious fever ... and could not eat, with pains in my side ...'[45]

The *Lord Melville* in a storm at sea

Though greatly weakened, he was able to enjoy the sights, but Jane was not there to comfort him:

> I gaze upon the city,
> A city new and strange;
> Down many a wat'ry vista
> My fancy takes a range
> From side to side I saunter,
> And wonder where I am; -
> And *can* you be in England,
> And I at Rotterdam?[46]

At least Hood was free, for a time, from his predatory creditors, but financial crises tend to have very rough edges. As might be expected, the required disposal of his assets entailed complicated negotiations. He wrote a very long letter to Jane in March 1835 mentioning that he hoped Reynolds (Jane's brother) 'may be able to beat the receivers about the house – it is hard to pay up after giving [£]100 for a lease.'[47]

> I am free to give my I.O.U,
> Sign, draw, accept as majors do,
> And free to lose my freedom too,
>   For want of due assets.[48]

On board ship, he had met a fellow-passenger, a young man named Vertue, whose family lived in Coblenz, 'so you see my morals are in good hands,' he wrote. Perhaps this fortuitous meeting persuaded him that Dilke's recommendation of Coblenz might be a pleasant enough place to settle in. But the journey to Coblenz was not without its problems.

The history of Germany, prior to Hood's arrival in 1835, had been one of tumult and aggression. The devastating war between Germany and France from 1793 to 1803 had had the effect of destabilising the old order. The Emperor lost the Netherlands, the Italian states and the vital territories west of the Rhine. In 1813, the War of Independence ended with the final defeat of the French at Leipzig and after the defeat of Napoleon in 1815, the Germanic Confederation was created. This major reorganisation of ill-matched states comprised Austria, Bavaria, Denmark, Hanover, Hesse, the Netherlands and Saxe-Coburg, and many others. A further conflict arose with a revolution in Brunswick, resulting in the flight of the Duke, and the abdication of the King of Saxony. Such confrontations continued and, on his way to Coblenz in 1835, Hood stopped at Nimegen to find himself in a war zone during the conflict between Belgium and Holland.

On arrival in Coblenz Hood booked himself into furnished rooms at 372 Kastorhof. There was a fine view over the Moselle, just below the point where it meets the Rhine, towards the impressive castle of Ehrenbreitstein on the hill. 'There are three little rooms,' he wrote, 'one backward, my study as is to be, with such a lovely view over the Moselle. My heart jumped when I saw it, and I thought, "There I shall write volumes!" '[49] Being well content with his new lodgings, he decided to send for Jane and the children: 'Get yourself strong, there is still a happy future; fix your eyes forward on our meeting, my best and dearest. Our little home, though homely, will be happy for us, and we do not bid England a very long good night.'[50]

Later, in the same letter, Hood gives Jane detailed instructions for the arduous journey to Coblenz, with the plan that he would meet her and children at Cologne:

> You must come to Rotterdam by "Der Batavier", which has female accommodations and a stewardess...The "Batavier" is an excellent boat; have *porter* on board her, as you will get none after Rotterdam; up the Rhine take Cognac and water, not the sour wine. Wrap yourself well up, and when the bustle of departure is over you may be very comfortable, but up to Cologne there is little worth seeing, except the towns, such as Düsseldorf. From Cologne to Coblenz is superb, and I shall enjoy it with you; but mind, be sure to come when you appoint, as I cannot stay long at Cologne.

View looking across the Moselle towards Ehrenbreitstein Castle, Coblenz, by Thomas Hood

Setting off on the *Batavier* on 29 March 1835, Jane duly arrived in early April with Tom and Fanny, and bringing with her a set of *Comic Annuals*, a bound copy of *The Athenaeum,* and a plentiful supply of woodblocks for his designs. They were met by Hood in Cologne. Jane could hardly recognise him. His emaciated appearance showed that his heart and lungs were seriously affected. His German doctor (who had read *Eugene Aram*) recommended him to convalesce at the spa town of Bad Ems, but Hood dared not spend precious funds at a time when the 1836 *Comic Annual* was already in preparation. They all stayed at the *Hotel du Rhin* in Cologne, and while there were impressed by a visit to the cathedral: 'The interior for lightness and elegance is perfectly exquisite… We saw all its wonders and relics, its golden shrine, inlaid with cameos and gems, and delicate mosaic,' Jane wrote in a letter to their doctor's wife, Mrs Elliot, a couple of months later.[51]

On the whole, Hood found the Germans too fond of smoking, guzzling and gourmandising to think of making friends with them – until one morning, when he was idly wandering through the streets of the town, he overheard a young army officer talking in English. He introduced himself as Lieutenant Philip de Franck of the 19th Polish Regiment of the German Army. De Franck's mother was English and he had been educated in England. Now, he was stationed across the Moselle at the fortress of Ehrenbreitstein. The Lieutenant visited him at Christmas and introduced him to the Christmas tree, then unknown in England. Jane served an English plum pudding, promising to make another for the Lieutenant. Thus began a most astonishing friendship – two kindred spirits, endowed with an identical, prankish sense of humour, which provided Hood with a rich fund of ideas for his German book. The Colonel of the Regiment was something of an intellectual and, to Hood's surprise, had published a worthy translation in German of *The Dream of Eugene Aram*. Hood had some concern about the clash of styles that might cause problems for the translator. He wrote to De Franck, 'I fear to ask about the translation of "Eugene Aram" it was in the most difficult style possible to translate into German; plain, almost Quaker-like; whereas German poetical style is flowery almost to excess.'[52]

Soon, at the colonel's invitation, Hood was delighted to accept a unique opportunity to accompany the regiment on a march to Bromberg in German Poland, taking place in the latter part of 1836. On his part, the colonel was honoured to have its famous author with him. For Hood, it was the opportunity to 'see parts of the country which are not common to travellers; he would have the advantage of very pleasant companions, and the help of Mr D Franck's German who speaks it as well as a native.'[53] So he was very glad to accept the invitation. Hood purchased a horse, complete with saddle and bridle, for £7 10s, and set out on a journey not without setbacks or amusing incident. This route-march began to form the basis for a new work in the style of Heads' *Brunnens*, but work on the *Comic Annual* had to come first. In Berlin, he indulged in a busy programme of sightseeing. Here, he was invited to dine with Prince Wilhelm Radziwill and his family, and was overjoyed to find they were already familiar with his work and had actually read his novel *Tylney Hall*.

Hood's son, Tom, records in *Memorials* that while in Germany, Hood bought a toy theatre for him and Fanny, and then (and subsequently at Camberwell) drew, painted and cut out the characters and scenery for a tragedy (Paul and Virginia), a spectacle (St George and the Dragon), and a pantomime. Hood was very ingenious with his hands, and creative in the way he would extemporise the dialogue. He also had a magic lantern, for which he painted a number of slides, some humorous and some pretty nature scenes.[54]

Four years later, on his eventual return to England, Hood received from De Franck a parcel containing two copies of a German translation of *The Dream of Eugene Aram*, translated into prose, this time by De Franck, and put into verse by Von Rühe – perhaps the very Colonel who had made the earlier version for the poem was published in 1841 at Bromberg. The German Preface claimed that the poem was superior to Bulwer-Lytton's novel of the same name, itself inspired by Hood's poem – 'Bulwer is a demi-god here.' The Preface further makes a claim for Hood as 'one of the first authors of modern England.' Von Rühe asked Hood to write to Prince Albert, enclosing the second copy together with his letter. Hood wrote:

> May it please Your Royal Highness, the greatest literary honour that can befal [*sic*] a poem is its translation into a foreign language, particularly the German. That such a distinction had been conferred on any verse of mine has only just been made known to me by the receipt of a volume from Bromberg. ... [B]eing thus unexpectedly brought under your Princely notice, let me crave permission to offer the respectful homage and loyal congratulations of the English author of 'Eugene Aram'.[55]

A reading of Hood's wry, whimsical and, at times, hilarious account of his stay in Germany, *Up the Rhine*, shows him to be decidedly British and that he had no inclination, nor indeed ability, to adapt to the local culture and language. On his return to London, however, in 1841, he admitted to De Franck that he understood 'twice as much German as I did in Germany, perhaps what I cropped there, has become digested by after-rumination, as the cows become more intimate with the cud.'[56] Snatches of German, mainly used for comic effect, show him to have learnt at least a smattering of day-to-day vocabulary and in his later letters to De Franck he uses German idioms in a natural manner as a laconic layer to his humour. In *Up the Rhine* (1840), farcical events occur as when Gradle [Gretel], a daily help, who knew only a few words of English is employed:

> Jane wanted fowl to boil for me. Now she has a theory that the more she makes her English un-English, the more it must be like German. Jane begins by showing Gradle a word in the dictionary.

> *Gradle*: "Ja! Yees –hühn –henne – ja! yees!"
> *Jane* (a little through her nose): "Hmn – hmn – hmn – yes – yaw – ken you geet a fowl –fool – foal, to boil – bile – bole for dinner?"
> *Gradle*: "Hot wasser?"
> *Jane*: "Yaw in pit – pat—pot –hmn – hum – eh?"
> *Gradle* (a little off-the-scent again): "Ja, nein – wasser, pot – hot – nein."
> *Jane*: "Yes – no – good to eeat – chicken – cheeken – checking – choking – bird – bard – beard – lays eggs – eeggs – hune, heine – hin – make cheekin broth – soup – poultry – peltry – paltry!"
> *Gradle* (quite at fault): "Pfeltrighchtch! [nonsense word] – nein."
> *Jane* (in despair): "What shall I do! and Hood won't help me, he only laughs. This comes of leaving England!" (She casts her eyes across the street at the Governor's poultry-yard, and a bright thought strikes her.) "here, Gradle – come here –comb hair – hmn – hum – look there –dare – you see things walking – hmn, hum, wacking about – things with feathers – fathers – feethers."
> *Gradle* (hitting it off again): "Feethers – faders – ah hah! Fedders – ja, ja, yees, sie bringen, fedders, ja, ja!"
> *Jane echoes*: "Fedders – yes – yaw, yaw!"
> Exit Gradle, and after three-quarters of an hour, returns triumphantly with two bundles of stationer's quills!!!
> Eventually the girl is dismissed with the words, 'On the First of February, March!' [57]

His correspondence too kept him extremely busy and he wrote long letters to Dilke, with whom he became a close friend. The Hood-Dilke correspondence is a study in itself, for it reveals Hood as a sensible family man, sincerely perplexed by the estrangement with the Reynolds family. It is also evident that Dilke found in Hood a kind and appreciative friend. Indeed, the Dilkes had visited the Hood family shortly before Hood joined De Franck's regiment for the march to Bromberg.

Meanwhile, Hood continued his battle with his creditors. He wrote to Dilke, in June 1836, a fuller account of his position as debtor:

> There were the menaces of the harsh & the requests of the gentle each equally urgent, may where all were just, the demand backed with kindness & consideration gave me most pain & inquietude. There was the agony of the Potent will & the impotent power. I believe I may say I was never a selfish debtor for I paid away money when I had it & left myself penniless almost, exposed to the mortification & deep annoyance for trifles. My struggles have been great & my sufferings unknown. … In spite of some sharp pangs in the process I am ready to confess that the crisis which sent me here was a wholesome one; I have been blamed I think not deservedly about Lake House, by Judges from the court, -- but the truth is my prospects & standing were latterly completely changed -- & I should have acted accordingly. … It is true I miss home – old friends – books, the communion of minds -- & I cannot I would not forget I am an Englishman. … I do hope in the bottom of my heart to return honourably to England'.[58]

Back in England, Hood's loyal and long-suffering engraver, John Wright, was carrying on the business of publishing the *Comic Annual* for 1836. Hood sent him copy and the completed wood-blocks from Coblenz but there were difficulties getting them through Customs. Hood was so relieved to shed the worries over the *Comic* that he celebrated the dispatch of the last box of drawings and manuscripts to England with a family supper.

There was no respite, however, for he had to set to work on the next *Comic Annual*, writing to Dilke, in June 1836, 'I am hard at work on my "Comic", somewhat puzzled for subjects, and most of my foreign ones must go to the German book, which I want to make as good as possible.' He sent his publisher, Alfred Head Baily, a correct list of Mottoes, for the Cuts, and a box of woodblocks, several to be engraved by John Scott. Baily's brother was intending to visit Hood but he never arrived, and Hood warned Baily not to allow the Cuts to be lost or fall into the hands of others. Then he found he had not sent enough and had to set to work again under great pressure – as he says, 'willy-nilly, well or illy!'[59]

This constant confusion of his 'honourable' concern for creditors and the resultant feeling of guilt, did not alleviate his weak physical condition following his return from Berlin. The march had been strenuous, too much for his frail and ailing body to sustain. Back in Coblenz, he developed a chronic cough and ended up spitting blood. The doctor was immediately sent for, and leeches applied, which rendered him even weaker still. A severe winter followed and Hood wrote of having 'a touch on the lungs'. But in spite of his health problems, there were many happy moments. There was hilarity over language difficulties. He related that Mrs Dilke had told him to get his linen well aired, having misunderstood 'Dampschiffe'* when on the river boats! Nevertheless, he set to work on the German book and, amazingly, despite delays, the *Comic Annual* for 1837 came out on time.

From Coblenz, Hood wrote a series of letters, about infringement of copyright, to the *Athenaeum,* entitled *Copyright and Copywrong*.[60] He had cause enough to attack the publishing world, as his financial ruin had been caused by an unsatisfactory relationship with his publisher. In those days, the law did little to protect the rights of authors and Hood wrote of 'the glorious uncertainty of the Law of Copyright' and suggested that 'an author will be obliged to repair to another country to enjoy his circulation'. He wrote:

> The question is not a mere sordid one – it is not a simple inquiry in what way the emoluments of literature may be best secured to the author of proprietors of a work; on the contrary, it involves a principle of grave importance, not only to literary men, but to those who love letters, – and, I will presume to say, to society at large. It has a moral as well as commercial bearing; for the Legislature will not have to decide directly, by a formal act, whether the literary interest is worthy of a place beside the shipping interest, and landed interest, the funded interest, the manufacturing, and other public interests, but also it will have indirectly to determine whether literary men belong to the privileged class, the higher, lower, or middle class, – the working class, – productive or unproductive class, – or in short, to any class at all.

He puts forward the following contingencies as expedients for fair treatment in business dealings between author and publisher:

---

* *Dampschiff* = Steamship

1st. In order that the author may know the true number of the impressions, and, consequently, the correct amount of the sale, it is necessary that his publishers should be honest. 2ndly. For the author to duly receive his profits, his publisher must be solvent.

This was a grim reflection on the state of affairs before eagerly awaited legislation was effected but Hood, being good natured and not having much of a head for business, continued to suffer at the hands of publishers such as Bailey and Colburn. As he so pertinently remonstrates in a second letter:

The liberty of the press is boasted of as part of the British constitution: but might it not be supposed that, in default of a censorship, some cunning Machiavel had devised a sly underplot for the discouragement of letters – an occult conspiracy to present 'men of learning and genius' to the world's eye in the pitiful plight of poor devils, starvelings, mumpers, paupers, vagrants, loose fish, jobbers, needy and seedy ones, nobodies, ne'er-do-wells, shy coves, strollers, creatures, wretches, objects, small debtors, borrowers, dependents, lack-pennies, half-sirs, clapper-dudgeons, scamps, insolvents, maunderers, blue-gowns, bedesman, scarecrows, fellows about town, sneaks, scrubs, shabbies, rascal deer among the herd.

At last, his struggle to finish *Up the Rhine* on time appeared to be coming to an end, but he complained once more to De Franck, in April 1837, 'I sent up two months ago a box full of sketches of my Rhine book … I half suspect the Rhinelanders opened my box going down, and were not best pleased at my Sketches of some of the dirty dandies hereabouts, which perhaps makes 'em so uncivil. Should all happen that I have wished to the Coblenzers in general. And the Douane in particular, the last ten days, they will be far from comfortable.'[61]

Hood's suspicions about the local townspeople were matched by his growing discontent with life in Coblenz itself. Inflammatory disorders did not suit his English blood. 'The man who bled me, and there are several bleeders here, told me he had attended eighty that month.'[62] Accordingly, having a longing to move nearer to home, Hood had the idea of moving to Ostend or Antwerp, possibly travelling via Cologne and Aix. He would be able to get over to England within a few hours, enabling him to be earlier with the next project. Posts would be more frequent, and take less time to arrive, so producing the forthcoming *Comic Annuals* would be much easier.

Before leaving, he visited, at De Franck's suggestion, one of his aristocratic German admirers, Prince Charles of Prussia, 3rd son of Friedrich Wilhelm III 1801-1883. He was surprised to find English prints, caricatures and other pictures adorning the walls of his private rooms and, on the table, he was delighted to find copies of the *Comic Annuals* - 'He is partial to us, and I entered my name in a book he keeps to know of his visitors.'

So, all was prepared for the leave-taking. As a parting gesture, the damp, murky climate of Coblenz presented them with a variety of colds and fevers to take with them on their journey. Everyone in the family contracted severe attacks of 'la grippe'. Fanny, at the height of her illness, had to endure leeches applied to her face, and young Tom suffered a discharge from his nose and ear. Hood's condition continued to be troublesome and debilitating, he was barely able to recover from the tensions and worries of overwork, the frustrations of coping with the complexities of publishing from abroad, all exacerbated by the exhausting effects of the strenuous route march to Berlin and back. Yet still he pursued, with an amazing subliminal kind of energy and spirit, the writing and preparations for printing his German book. Hood's life was one long battle between his endemic sickness and frailty and the exigencies of his chosen profession, for in spite of physical weakness on a daily basis, he found a remarkable inner strength that carried him through one crisis after another. He deserved more from life than it gave him in return and yet his faith in the dignity of authorship was matchless. There is all the pity and the wonder in his brave, spirited response to the ever-challenging conditions under which he served his chosen master – the Book Trade.

Hood would have been incapable of managing his publishing affairs over in London without the help of Wright, who worked from his premises near Fenchurch Street in the City of London. He and his partner, Robert Branston, had engraved the portrait of Thomas Rounding, Master of the Essex Hunt, mounted on his horse, Spankaway, as a frontispiece for Hood's roisterous poem, *The Epping Hunt*, published by Charles Tilt in 1829. Branston also engraved many of the woodcuts for the early *Comic Annuals* and was on fairly intimate terms with Hood. He had occupied Lake House, Wanstead, after Hood's financial collapse. According to Jane Hood, following his bankruptcy in 1833, Branston went into partnership with Wright, who continued to engrave for the *Annuals* and to help Hood directly with his publishing ventures, which were by no means eased by the pressing need to communicate regularly across the North Sea.

A revealing letter to Wright in April 1837 tells of some of the difficulties Hood encountered with his then publisher, Alfred Head Baily, with whom Hood was beginning to fall out. A letter specifically marked 'Private' - so that Baily would not open it, though he may well have been tempted to do so in the circumstances - asks Wright to be cautious about spreading news of the seriousness of Hood's present state of health less the already weak state in the confidence of his remaining creditors be exacerbated. In the interests of publishing history and the purpose of this account of Hood's life, it is worth quoting this crucial letter at some length:

'The reason I want you to keep it to yourself is in case Baily should take any fright & suppose I am in a bad way. The truth is your first letter scared me, by informing me that the cuts were above a month in going – for in that case every set of cuts would take a month to draw – a month to go -- & and a month to cut = 3 months! Enough, with the best of health, to neutralize any efforts to be early. I was meditating a move therefore on this sole account, the difficulty of communication -- & you may suppose the passage of the blocks here with the blocks I wanted, above a month again, only confirmed this necessity. But in the interim, whilst it was coming – I was again seized with a spitting of blood – only six weeks after the one before – which, being serious to apprehend if repeated so – set me thinking of searching whether the climate here itself is not at fault. ... The illness has hindered my German book of course, but if you calculate, had I been well, it couldn't have been ready for May. I only got the fresh blocks on the 14 April -- & if I had sent them instantly blank you wouldn't get them till the 14th May – allowing me no time to draw nor you to cut them. I do not see the possibility then of being ready for June – the more the pity. But I shall not lose an hour. And I do not see the injury of one to the other book in the same half year – but think they may be made to help each other – by good manifestoes etc – supposing both are early & one a month or two before the other. ... I am glad you liked the drawings. You are right about them – they will require engraving – and I should like them well done. They are not like comic cuts mere jokes – but portraits – facsimiles of the people etc & should be correctly done. I hope to make it altogether a superior book. I shall have another set of good ones to send you. You may show them to Hervey if you like. ... I had a rare bother about the box with the Customs. It had been opened at the frontier & they wanted to open it again here. But I beat 'em. Some wet had got in & the blocks almost wet, & one of the bindings was a little stained by damp...[63]

Baily deeply annoyed Hood, purposely pre-empting the publication of *Up the Rhine* by bringing out a rival book entitled *A Guide Up the Rhine* by Francis Coghlan* (to whom Hood refers as 'Ughlan'!) in 1837, three years before the much-delayed issue of Hood's account in 1840. [64] Coghlan's book was a straightforward detailed assemblage of useful information for the traveller; it was no match for Hood's semi-fictional account of his Rhineland experiences, with all its farcical episodes, its preponderance of jokes and puns, and its often beguiling humorous descriptions. In fact, Hood had nothing whatsoever to fear from any competition, for he had, through dint of hard work, long hours, and against all odds, had succeeded in turning his situation to advantage. He wrote to his doctor, William Elliott, in June 1837, '… should the new Copyright Act pass I have perhaps acquired something though not immediately available – but as I had before now made as much in one year as would cancel all my liabilities, I see no reason to despair of yet returning to England (health allowing) in a year or two.'[65]

Before leaving for Belgium, Hood had begun work on his protest at the inadequacies of copyright law in England, and became seriously concerned about what Isaac D'Israeli referred to as 'the calamities of authors'. Sergeant Talfourd, Charles Dickens, and Thomas Carlyle took up the cudgel in defence of the large number of writers of all kinds, who had been forced into exile, or worse, suffered the humiliations of the Debtors' Prison.

Since 1585, every book published had to be licensed by law, and the title, author and publisher recorded in the records of Stationer's Hall in London. In 1649, an Ordinance was issued under Queen Anne forbidding the printing of any work without the consent of the owner, but it was a further sixty years before authors could have their writings protected for 14 years. The concept of perpetual copyright was over-ruled by the House of Lords in 1774, though Hood wholeheartedly supported it when he came to publish his three 'Letters', or essays, on the subject, *Copyright and Copywrong*. Later Acts extended the rights to 28 years, then for the life-time of the author, and finally to extend further to seven years after death. The issue had to wait to be resolved until 1842, with Talfourd's Act, passed by Parliament just three years before Hood's death. It took well over 150 years for other types of printing, such as engravings, prints, musical compositions, designs and photographs, to be protected for 70 years after death. Thus the 'calamities of authors' were largely over, or were they?

Sir Thomas Noon Talfourd (1795-1854), a Sergeant at Law, and the enthusiastic proposer of the Copyright Act was on friendly terms with

---

* Francis Coghlan (b. Dublin 1806). Author of many travel books, including *A Guide Up the Rhine, from London, to Rotterdam, the Hague, Amsterdam, Cologne; Dover, Calais, and Antwerp.*

Wordsworth, Coleridge, and Hood's close friend, Charles Lamb. He had published a volume of poetry, composed a successful tragedy, and contributed to Baily's *New Monthly Magazine* and the *Retrospective Review,* though it is more likely that Hood came to know him in the early days of the *London Magazine.* Talfourd, as a Member of Parliament for Reading for 1835, 1837, and 1841, introduced his most important contribution to the political agenda, his Copyright Bill, which proposed 60 years of protection, thus allowing immediate beneficiaries to benefit from his labours. Accordingly, Hood signed a Petition with 32 other authors, which was brought before Parliament, by Talfourd, on 27 February 1839. His own petition, however, was not presented as it was considered to contain points of humour in places, thus weakening the power of his argument and rendering it unsuitable for the solemnity of the subject. Nevertheless, Talfourd understood the passion of Hood's intention and, in spite of their official rejection, the 'Letters' were published in *The Athenaeum* [66].

The first letter reflects on the low status of authors in the eyes of the law: 'We are on a par …with quack doctors, street-preachers, strollers, ballad-singers, hawkers of last dying speeches, Punch-and-Judies, conjurors, tumblers, and other vagabonds. … We are by law – outlaws, undeserving of civil rights.' He goes on to say that 'Writers have no protection against piracy, not only abroad but in their land; they are prey to dishonest publishers and booksellers.' The second letter deliberates on the literary worth of a writer and how neglected he is, bereft of public recognition and honours, his works considered, if at all, 'as a vanity or luxury than as a grand moral engine, capable of advancing the spiritual interest of mankind.' In the last letter, he dwells on the public perception of authors as eccentrics and libertines, their unfortunate heirs unable to benefit from his genius.

Not all booksellers were as scheming and predatory as those Hood encountered along life's way. Some, like Byron's publisher, John Murray, were generous and sympathetic when called upon to help, as letters to him from Hood might suggest. Hood's cogent argument in favour of the dignity of authorship was expressed with fervour born of his bitter struggle to survive in the cut-throat world of publishing, and made a deep impression on his fellow writers, Dickens and Thackeray. Through the wit and the jesting, there is wise counsel for politicians that presages Hood's powerful empathy with the downtrodden and underprivileged parts of the social order. He broke through barriers and made everyone listen, from the poorest to the richest, from the beggars and ballad-sellers of Seven Dials who sang his verses in the streets, to German princes – and even the King of England himself.

As Hood and his family set off for Ostend in hope and expectation, there was the worry that the freight to Rotterdam may have been doubly paid in error by both Baily and Hood who could ill-afford such wastage of funds and might have to accept the loss. The family settled in at 39 Rue Longue towards the end of June 1837. Hood benefited from the fresh sea breezes and his breathing and general health began to improve. As he recounts:

> 'The Esplanade is very fine, and the sands famous for our brats, who delight in them extremely. We munch shrimps morning and night, as they are very abundant, and quite revel in the fish. I have dined several days on nothing else, and it is such a comfort to think of only that strip of sea between us, quick communications by packets, and posts four times a week, that I feel quite in spirits as to my work, and hopeful as to my health. ... The King and Queen of Belgium come here in a fortnight; so that I shall be the neighbour of royalty, as they will live in our street, only three or four doors off. '[67]

99

Chapter 10 - A Man of Principle

With the Hood family newly settled in Ostend, Hood was feeling more optimistic about his work, and began work immediately on the *Comic Annual* for 1838. Now, acquaintances from England could visit them, and it was not long before their old friends, the Dilkes, came, and a more than welcome visit from Wright, the loyal manager of his business; publishing details could be at last discussed at first hand. Hood was thankful that the Cuts could take under six weeks to process. He had become much more the man of business than many would give him credit for. Among the countless debtors, many of them English, he met Colley Grattan.* Like Hood, Grattan had had to leave England in 1828 because of financial losses, and had now been in Ostend for some years before their meeting. Apart from their shared experiences of exile, Hood was able to lend Grattan some letters from Charles Lamb that he had with him.

But he was not to know that the severe winter in Coblenz had already sealed his fate. He was now a prematurely aged man. Letters written by his wife reveal his vain but valiant struggle to overcome ill health and the almost uncanny strength of his cheerful philosophy. Moving to Ostend proved at least temporarily beneficial, as contact with London was made easier by the four posts a week. 'We are very comfortable here.' he wrote to his doctor, 'Fanny is quite improved in health, getting flesh and colour, and Tom is health itself. Mrs Hood, too, fattens, and looks well. I have got through more this year than since I have been abroad.'[68]

With the coronation in the news, Hood contemplated writing an Ode to Queen Victoria for *The Athenaeum* and noted: 'Why can't the Queen make me Consul here? I don't want to turn anybody out, but can't there be nothing-to-do enough for two?' Early in that year, Hood was working on a new project, that of collecting together all his contributions to the *Comic Annuals* and reissuing them in monthly instalments: 'I do not think I fall off and have no misgivings about overwriting myself. I hear a demon whisper – I hope no lying one – I can do better yet, or as good as ever, and more of it; so let's look for the best. Nobody ever died the sooner for hoping it.'

Hood was ultimately concerned with the contemporary scene: firstly through the universal experience of everyday life – all the cant, hypocrisy, and stuffiness; then through current events such as the burning down of the House of Commons, the construction of a Thames tunnel, the sensational ascent in a balloon, and firework displays at Vauxhall Gardens. He

---

* Thomas Colley Grattan (1732-1864), the author of the popular *Highways and Byways* (1823), an account of his tours in France, later British Consul in Boston during the settlement of the American northern border question.

preoccupied himself with the iniquities of industrialisation, the dangers of gin-drinking, and the abolition of the slave trade. In his poetry we find politicians, parsons, kings, writers, inventors, domestic servants, quack doctors, actors and aeronauts, to name but a few. He was quick to appreciate the significance of events; hardly had news appeared, than he was scratching out a diatribe against Sabbatarians like Sir Andrew Agnew* and Rae Wilson, or praising prison-reformer Elizabeth Fry and Sir Walter Scott with an ode. He was responsible, too, for extending the scope and subject matter of poetry, which, by conventional standards, he frequently treated irreverently. He infused the sonnet and the ode, hitherto considered as serious verse forms, with wit and irony and produced such masterly pieces as the *Sonnet to Vauxhall,* which begins:

> The cold transparent ham is on my fork –
> It hardly rains – and hark the bell! – ding-dingle –
> Away! Three thousand feet at gravel work,
> Mocking a Vauxhall shower! – Married and Single
> Crush – rush; – Soak'd Silks with wet white Satin mingle.
> Hengler! Madame! Round whom all bright sparks lurk,
> Calls audibly on Mr. and Mrs. Pringle
> To study the Sublime, &c. (vide Burke)
> All Noses are upturn'd! – Whish – ish! – On high
> The rocket rushes – trails – just steals in sight –
> Then droops and melts in bubbles of blue light –
> And darkness reigns – Then balls flare up and die –
> Wheels whiz – smack crackers – serpents twist – and then
> Back to the cold transparent ham again! [69]

Just as publishers came under fire from his wit, so politicians were the victims of his spleen, especially when the liberty of the individual was at stake. In 1812, Spencer Percival, the Prime Minister, had delivered a speech to the House on the need for a day of fasting and forgiveness, to which Hood replied with this ode:

> Whatever others do, – or don't,
> I cannot – dare not – must not feast, and won't
> Unless by night your day you let me sleep,
> And *fast* asleep; [70]

---

* Sir Andrew Agnew, 7th Baronet (1793-1849), politician and staunch supporter of Sunday Sabbatarianism.

Agnew, author of the Lord's Day Observance Bill, was also the subject of a bitter ode on the dullness of the English Protestant Sunday, a subject which would have pleased Lamb:

> Six days made all that is, you know, and then
> Came that of rest – by holy ordination,
> As if to hint unto the sons of men,
> After creation should come re-creation.
> Read right this text, and do no further search
> To make a Sunday Workhouse of the Church. [ll. 100-105][71]

At Ostend, Hood completed the *Ode to Rae Wilson*, a poem that revealed Hood as being seriously concerned with religious controversy and reflected sincere and 'engaged' criticism of earlier odes, but expressed his views with far greater mastery of technique. The ode sets out to expose the hypocritical attitude to religion that Wilson, who had attacked Hood on several occasions regarding his beliefs, expressed in his books. Irritated by Wilson's sermonising, Hood makes a plea for a simple religion, free from the control of parliament, relying far more on the individual conscience:

> How much a man can differ from his neighbour:
> One wishes worship freely giv'n to God,
> Another wants to make it statute labour –
> The broad distinction in a line to draw,
> As means to lead us to the skies above,
> You say – Sir Andrew* and his love of law,
> I say – the Saviour with his law of love. [ll. 109-114]

> Say, was it to my spirit's gain or loss,
> One bright and balmy morning, as I went
> From Liege's lovely environs to Ghent,
> If hard by the wayside I found a cross,
> That made me breathe a pray'r upon the spot –
> While Nature of herself as if to trace
> The emblem's use, had trail'd around its base
> The blue significant Forget-Me-Not?
> Methought, the claims of Charity to urge
> More forcibly, along with Faith and Hope,
> The pious choice had pitch'd upon the verge
> Of a delicious slope,
> Giving the eye much variegated scope;

---

* Sir Andrew Agnew

'Look round,' it whispered,
'On that prospect rare,
Those vales so verdant, and those hills so blue;
Enjoy the sunny world, so fresh, and fair,
But' – (how the simple legend pierc'd me thro)
'PRIEZ POUR LES MALHEUREUX.' [ll. 290-307][72]

In revolt against the gloomy religion of the old Calvinism and the new Evangelism, Hood here asserts his own religious and intellectual freedom. His war against cant, which he regarded as the worst enemy of Christianity, continued to the end of his life.

In 1838, *Hood's Own* began to appear in instalments under the full title: *Hood's Own; or Laughter from Year to Year: being Former Runnings of His Comic Vein, with an Infusion of New Blood for General Circulation.* Its success did not counterbalance the effects of continuous work at his desk, and the ardours of a cold bleak winter. Hood's health steadily declined, though his condition was concealed from family and friends by an irrepressible desire to pun and joke away the pain. In January 1839, he crossed over to England with the purpose of again consulting his friend and physician, Dr Elliot, on the advisability of remaining in Ostend for another year or two, noting in a letter: 'It will be sometime before I shall be strong enough to live a London life; and being rather popular in that city, I cannot keep out of society and late hours.' In Samuel Carter Hall's description: 'His countenance had more of melancholy than of mirth; it was calm even in solemnity. There was seldom any conscious attempt at brilliancy in his talk; and so far from sharing in that weakness, with which wits are generally credited, a desire to monopolise the conversation, he seemed ever ready in society to give way to any who would supply talk.'[73] This seems to be true, for Thackeray confirmed it in a reminiscence: 'I quite remember his pale face; he was thin and deaf, and very silent; he scarcely opened his lips during dinner, and he made one pun'.

While in England, Hood took the opportunity of going through the accounts with his publisher. The situation seemed promising, for though other periodicals were disappearing from the market, his own remained popular. The *Comic Annual* had maintained its reputation. Dr Elliot's diagnosis of liver trouble disturbed Hood greatly, but he was considerably relieved to hear that his lungs were stronger. In a letter to De Franck, he wrote: 'I shall never be strong again – Jane got the verdict of our friend Dr. Elliot, that the danger of the case has gone, but that as I had never been particularly strong and sturdy, I must not now expect to be more than a young old gentleman.' The variability of the English climate upset him: 'We are all a little rabid at present, for after having fires far into June, the weather has just set in broiling hot, and the children do not know what to make of it' ' But the inclemency of Ostend was no better, for he later complains: 'What an abominable swindling season! The winter embezzled the spring, and the summer has absconded with the autumn'.

By the end of the year, *Hood's Own* was ready, as well as the *Comic Annual* for 1839. Hood referred to the preparation of the *Annual* as 'a long miracle', a remark that he further elaborates in a letter written on his 40th birthday (23 May 1839) to De Franck, in which he says: 'I am only able to write at short length, having more work for my pen and less time to do it in than ever. I have had a sad nine or ten months of it, almost always ill, and then having to do everything in haste by day and night. I think my liver complaint is tolerably cured, and I have not spit any blood for a very long while, but the curing has half-killed me. I am as thin as a lath and as weak as plaster'.[74] A certain note of cynicism creeps into a remark that the first 40 years of his life are like 'The Forty Thieves; having stolen away all my youth and health'. He allows himself a small joke or two at De Franck's expense, for after another serious illness, he had lost all his hair – a joke that shows the very thin dividing line between humour and unintentional cruelty.

On their return to Ostend, Jane took Hood's business matters in hand, preferring to travel to England herself rather than to subject him to the rigours of crossing the North Sea in winter, and possibly because she remembered the disastrous voyage to Rotterdam just over four years before. Once, during her absence, Hood suffered a severe attack, whimsically recalling the experience thus: 'It was CRUEL suffering; but I could not describe, without laughing, that cramp, for I was pirouetting about on one leg, and the other drawn up in such a twist, as only Grimaldi used to effect'.

Just before Christmas, he published his volume of reminiscences *Up the Rhine*,[75] the first edition of which sold out within a fortnight. It is undoubtedly his finest prose work, and has its roots ion the occasional pieces, *Sketches On and Off the Road*. Although in parts inspiration flags, the volume contains some of the best characterisation in the whole of his work. The book is in the form of letters written by members of a touring party travelling up the Rhine valley. The letters reveal not only the inner thoughts of the characters, but also recount incidents in which one or more of them had been involved, told from different points of view.

Hood had frequently adopted this means of telling a story, and took great delight in the inclusion of an illiterate person in the party as a butt for his incisive humour. One thinks of the irresponsible schoolboy in *The Pugsley Papers* at the beginning of *Hood's Own*. In *Up the Rhine,* there is clumsy, vague, emotional Martha, whose letters, with their simplified spelling and naïve vacancy, are perhaps the most delightful. She rambles on about her suitors, her inability to cope with the language, and her sudden and dramatic conversion to Roman Catholicism. The predicaments and squabbles of touring parties have not changed in over a 100 years if we are to believe Hood's account of *Up the Rhine*. The description of food, countryside, fellow travellers, cathedrals and adventures of this curiously assorted group come to life in this delightful book, wavering between the sublime and the ridiculous with an equanimity that reveals a broadening technical ability and a deepening understanding of human idiosyncrasies.

The success of *Up the Rhine* was small comfort to a man as sick as Hood. He had begun to quarrel with his publisher, Alfred Head Baily, over financial agreements, which resulted in a prolonged legal battle destined to drag on after Hood's death. During the remainder of his life, and especially at this time, it had a serious effect on his general health. The sale of his books was badly affected until a temporary agreement was reached and good relations were restored more by mutual condescension than by goodwill. The dismal winter was made worse by the death of his friend, Wright, the engraver, with whom he had been in constant touch over the publication of the *Comic Annual*.

The trouble with Baily compelled him once more to visit England on business. He had also had an invitation to stay at Dr Elliot's house in Stratford, Essex. Jane was wisely advised to acquiesce. The dampness of the climate in Ostend had not improved the condition of his lungs. There was mention of a removal to Dieppe. He was ordered to speak as little as possible and remarked: 'I will try to be as dumb as I can; but then I have so many impediments to silence as there are sometimes to speech.' His sickness often took unexpected turns for the worse. On arrival at Dr Elliot's house in Stratford, Hood suffered an attack of blood-spitting, aggravated, as he put it, to 'a largeness of my heart', and he described himself as 'a sort of melodramatic mystery'.[76] In fact, Dr Elliot was to confide to Jane in a letter written the following month, that 'your husband is suffering from organic disease of the heart – an enlargement and thickening of it – with contraction of the valves, and from haemorrhage from the lungs, or spitting of blood, recurring very frequently. There is also disorder of the liver and the stomach, aggravated by the nature of his pursuits...' in other words, the stress caused by having to meet publishers' deadlines.[77]

Some days later, he wrote that, during his stay with Dr Elliot for recuperation, he had had a ride out for the first time, with the doctor, passing within sight of his former residence, Lake House, Wanstead: 'I bore the sight of Lake House very well till passing the front and looking up at that bedroom window; the recollection of so much misery suffered there came over me like a cloud.'[78] No wonder the sight of the house brought sad recollections, as it was here that his wife had become so ill just after the birth of their son, Tom, striking the first blow to Hood's prosperity. Elliot pressed Hood to return to England permanently and to avoid overstraining his mental and physical powers.

106

Chapter 11 - Social Conscience

The strain of financial insecurity and increasing responsibilities in family and profession weakened Hood's resistance, making the last five years of his life a tale of patient endurance in his fight against physical pain. Paradoxically, they were years which produced his strongest and most original work. He began a new series for the *New Monthly Magazine,* entitled *Rhymes for the Times and Reason for the Season*, which included the poem *An Open Question*, concerning the closing of the Zoological Gardens on Sundays. Hood's view of the English Sunday had been admirably expressed in the odes to Agnew and Wilson, and were not unlike Lamb's view expressed in his essay, *The Superannuated Man* [79]:

> There is a gloom for me attendant upon a city Sunday, a weight in the air. I miss the cheerful cries of London, the music, and the ballad-singers – the buzz and stirring murmur of the streets. Those eternal bells depress me. The closed shops repel me.

Hood objected to religion being cast into a Puritanical gloom, for divine worship was not contingent on repression of the joy of living; Sunday was a day of rest, perhaps, but must never be observed in the spirit of mourning to which the Church subjected it.

In September 1840, he published his most original work to date: *Miss Kilmansegg and Her Precious Leg*, a contribution to the *New Monthly Magazine*. It is subtitled 'A Golden Legend' and is, in effect, a novel in verse. It concerns the pedigree, birth, christening, childhood, education, courtship, marriage, misery and murder of a fictitious Miss Kilmansegg. From the very beginning of her life she is surrounded by the glint and glimmer of gold; an affluent ancestor is not forgotten:

> Gold! And Gold! And gold without end!
> He had gold to lay by, and gold to spend,
> Gold to give, and gold to lend,
> And reversions of gold in future.
> In wealth the family revell'd and roll'd;
> Himself and wife and sons so bold;
> And his daughters sang to their harps of gold
> 'O bella étà del'oro!'

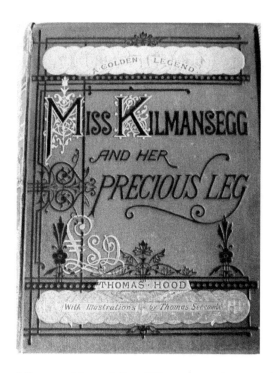

Following a riding accident, Miss Kilmansegg loses a leg, and not surprisingly chooses an artificial one of solid gold. At a ball she meets a spurious foreign count, with whom she falls in love and subsequently marries. The honeymoon is ominously lit by the silver light of the moon, just as her birth had been overshadowed by a silver spoon. She is ultimately murdered by her husband, who hits her over the head with her golden leg. At his trial, he is acquitted on the grounds that, since Miss Kilmansegg had died by a blow from her own leg, it was a case of suicide. The poem stems from Hood's early ballads, with their grimness and farce, touched by the seriousness of *Aram,* and is finely sustained in its ingenious rhymes, and in the urgency and sense of doom which the metre evokes. The originality of the conception and treatment are unsurpassed. Though it is a fundamentally humorous poem, it had a message which could not fail to cut into the heart of the materialistic society of the times. It was a bitter satire of the age, conceived with an understanding of contemporary values. Browning, in *Toccata at Galuppi's,* speaks of earthly pleasures, but, in *Miss Kilmansegg and Her Precious Leg* Hood reveals the dangers of attaching too much importance to the love of money. He drives right to the root of a social problem that he sees as one of the most dangerous to a growing economy. The poem is notable for its style and inspiration but also for its characterisation. The description of the parents at the christening is masterly:

To paint the maternal Kilmansegg
The pen of an Eastern Poet would beg,
And need an elaborate sonnet;
How she sparkled with gems whenever she stirr'd
And her head niddle-noddled at every word,
And seem'd so happy, a Paradise Bird
Had nidificated upon it.

And Sir Jacob the Father strutted and bow'd,
And smiled to himself, and laugh'd aloud,
To think of his heiress and daughter –
And then in his pockets he made a grope,
And then, in the fullness of joy and hope,
Seem'd washing his hands with invisible soap
In imperceptible water.

Soon after the publication of *Miss Kilmansegg and her Precious Leg*, *Tylney Hall* was reissued with a new preface in Bentley's series of Standard Novels. The sale of the copyright enabled the Hoods to return to England permanently. They settled in lodgings in Camberwell, a part of London later associated with Ruskin and Browning. Hood's popularity was spreading, not only in England but in Germany too, where De Franck had collaborated with von Rühe in a further translation of *The Dream of Eugene Aram* into German, a copy having been presented to the Prince Consort; Hood wrote to De Franck and gratefully remarks: 'For your sake I will not regret Germany'.[80]

From time to time, the Committee of the Royal Literary Fund consulted Dilke as to Hood's health and the progress of the 'Baily business', subsequently voting Hood the sum of £50. He needed the money desperately, but proudly declined the offer, returning it with the utmost respect, explaining that he hoped to overcome all his troubles 'as independently as heretofore'.

Punch was started in 1841. The first issue contained a slighting reference to Hood, that suggests that the sponsors were not in favour of his popularity: 'Mr. Hood, Professor of Punmanship, begs to acquaint the dull and witless, that he has established a class for the acquirement of an elegant and ready style of punning, on the pure Joe Millerian principle. The very worst hands are improving in six short and mirthful lessons....A good laughter wanted.' It was an astute bid for power – an attempt to win over the interest and support of the magazine-reading public from one who had been in the business for many years. Hood objected to having his name used in such a manner, and was undoubtedly vexed by the fact that *Punch* claimed originality in attacking the very faults and vices of society and weaknesses of human nature which he himself had been fighting against in his odes. He would have to wait for two years to impress his genius on a fickle public, and to become the dominant force in the sphere of social criticism in verse.

In the meantime, the editor of the *New Monthly Magazine*, Theodore Hook, died, and Colburn, the publisher, offered the editorship to Hood at £100 a year less than Hook had been receiving. Hood firmly refused. Colburn then promised the correct salary of £300. By September the matter was settled. The new post, which Hood now assumed, gave Jane a new lease of life. The family moved to St John's Wood, where they took rooms in Elm Tree Road, overlooking Lord's Cricket Ground, which Hood felt to be a serious drawback, for when he was at work he could often see others at play. With regular work on the magazine and his former anxieties relieved by a steady salary, his health improved – at least temporarily. There were simple dinner parties, and occasional visits to the Dilkes, who had their summer cottage at Twickenham.

Early in 1842, Hood decided to revive the *Comic Annual*, as there had been a resurgence of magazines and periodicals. In the summer of the same year, he was one of a group of friends who gave Dickens a welcome-home celebration at Greenwich on his return from America, when the party dined on turtle soup, whitebait and champagne. By now Dickens and Hood were on intimate terms and Hood was writing reviews of Dickens' *American Notes* in the *New Monthly Magazine* , and went so far as to suggest a motto for a new work: 'I wish I was in A-me-ri-ca!'[81] – words that Coleridge was frequently wont to exclaim in his Pantisocracy days.

Just three weeks before Christmas, Hood received a visit from Dickens, accompanied by his wife and sister-in-law, but there is no detailed record of the visit. There were other visitors too: Henry Crabb Robinson, the lawyer and diarist, for example, records calling on Mary Lamb, who had only just recovered from one of her depressive states, and found her 'quite in possession of her faculties, and recollecting everything nearly', and walked with her to St John's Wood where he left her at the Hoods' home.

Chapter 12 - The Uncrowned Laureate

Douglas Jerrold's *Cakes and Ale* appeared in this year with a dedication to Hood '... whose various genius touches alike the springs of laughter and the source of tears' – a tribute closely reminiscent of Walter Savage Landor's:

> Before me on each path there stood
> The witty and the tender Hood.

In March 1843 Southey died, and the question arose as to who would be his successor as Poet Laureate. Hood wrote to Dilke asking what the chances were of his being appointed but it was unlikely that a comic poet would be afforded the honour of becoming the Queen's own poet. This must have rankled Hood considerably since his innermost thoughts were directed towards serious writing. At this time, he had come to the end of a period of comic verse which had established him in the eyes of many as the Grimaldi of literature and nothing could undo that reputation. Had Southey lived another year, Hood may well have stood a chance of receiving the laureateship. Indeed, to his many admirers, Hood seemed a likely candidate, but a 'comic' author was not thought to possess sufficient dignity. Had he lived in the age of Betjeman (a great admirer), Hood would undoubtedly been chosen for the position. Browning and Tennyson had only just begun to publish their best work. The greatest of the established poets was William Wordsworth and it was natural that he should be offered the post. But we can only wonder with what poetic *tours de force*, with what sublime comicalities, Hood would have entertained his adoring readers. He would certainly have been delighted with his public role and no doubt would have poured forth a torrent of memorable verbal pyrotechnics to prove it.

The year was a busy one for Hood. He wrote to De Franck: 'The hardest work is writing refusals to literary ladies, who <u>will</u> write poetry, and <u>won't</u> write it well. I wish you would come and marry a few of them, which would perhaps reduce them to prose'.[82] In spite of pressure of work, Hood managed to take a short holiday in September 1843, and set out with his son, Tom, to visit some of the haunts of his youth from some 30 years earlier. He visited his ageing aunt in Tayport, afterwards going on to Dundee, where he made daily visits to places he had known as a boy. A further week was spent in Edinburgh, sightseeing most of the time. Looking longingly up at Salisbury Crags and Arthur's Seat, he sighed: 'Who can tell how hard it is to climb? I don't think I shall manage it, but mean to try some cool evening'.[83]

On his return to London, his general health seemed greatly improved but no sooner had he arrived than he received news, concerning two volumes of the *New Monthly Magazine* he was preparing, of 'tedious waitings on Colburn', with hints of friction in discussions over unfair terms of contract. Hood consulted Dickens, who replied in scathing words: 'There can be no doubt in the mind of any honourable man, that the circumstances under which you signed your agreement are of the most disgraceful kind in so far as Mr Colburn is concerned.... he took a money-lending, bill-broke, Jew-clothes-bagging, Saturday-night-pawn-broking advantage of your temporary situation.' Not long after, Hood complained: '...my fortunes seem subject to crisis, like certain disorders'. One of these crises arose over the publication of his poem, *A Drop of Gin*, which he contributed to the November number of *Punch*. Although it was a temperance tract, objections were made to the propriety of the expression. The poem begins:

> Gin! Gin! A Drop of Gin!
> What magnified Monsters circle therein!
> Ragged, and stained with filth and mud,
> Some plague-spotted, and some with blood!

This 'liquor of Sin', he says, consumed in seedy gin palaces, leads to poverty, misery and ultimately to complete destitution. The poem ends with a doomful message:

> Gin! Gin! a Drop of gin!
> Oh! then its tremendous temptations begin,
> To take, alas!
> To the fatal glass, –
> And happy the wretch that it does not win
> To change the black hue
> Of his ruin to blue –
> While Angels sorrow, and Demons grin –
> And lose the rheumatic
> Chill of his attic
> By plunging into the Palace of Gin!

It is difficult now to see why objections were made to the poem since its overall tone is one of condemnation – a warning to the poor that alcohol was the way to ruin and loss of self- respect, and was a dangerous panacea for the pangs of an empty stomach.

The appearance of the Christmas number of *Punch* on 16 December 1843 altered Hood's life and assured him a permanent place in the annals of literature and sociology in England and abroad. In the previous October, a seamstress named Biddell was charged at Lambeth police court with pawning articles belonging to her employer. She was a poor widow with a family of children to feed and clothe. During the interrogation she revealed that she was able to earn only seven shillings a week and it was subsequently stated that her employer considered this to be a living wage. The case provoked indignation in all sections of society. Two days later *The Times* published a strongly-worded leader on the incident, which was taken up and quoted in *Punch* in an article entitled *Famine and Fashion*, with bitter critical additions. Hood was so moved by the injustice and suffering that the woman had endured, that he sat down and wrote one of his most famous and inspired poems. He showed it to Jane and as it was being wrapped up she remarked: 'Now mind, Hood, mark my words, this will tell wonderfully! It is one of the best things you ever did!'

Mark Lemon, editor of *Punch* at the time, revealed that the author had enclosed a covering letter explaining that he had already sent the poem to three newspapers, that it had been rejected by them and that he was afraid it was not suitable for publication in *Punch*. Jane's confidence in its future success was borne out by events. *The Song of the Shirt* became the most fêted poem of the year. It was reprinted in *The Times*, among many other papers and journals, and translated into many languages. Hood wondered whimsically how French and German writers would render 'Stitch, stitch, stitch!' and how 'Seam and gusset and band!' would sound in Dutch. The poem was printed on scarves and handkerchiefs, sung in the streets by the poor to a tune of their own and, some 50 years later, in 1906, it was read at the West Hampstead Unitarian Church in place of the Second Lesson, the sermon on that occasion being concerned with sweated labour. The poem took its place in popular literature as something of a folk song, for it was near to the heart and conscience of the nation. Its publication trebled the circulation of *Punch* and sealed Hood's fame. Published anonymously, there was considerable speculation as to its authorship. Anyone familiar with *The Dream of Eugene Aram* or *Miss Kilmansegg and her Precious Leg* would have soon discovered the secret and it was Dickens who guessed the answer to the riddle. A number of people claimed it as their own work and Hood was finally compelled to reveal his identity publicly.

The editorship of the *New Monthly Magazine* now become a burden to him. Colburn resented Hood's new-found fame and, since the work was demanding and the post unremunerative, Hood resigned. Colburn's resentment grew to such proportions that he returned three letters addressed to Hood with the endorsement: 'Not known to Mr. Colburn'. Hood's sudden rise to worldwide fame served only to aggravate his physical condition and his health once more began to decline. Charles Cowden Clarke, on meeting Hood at a friend's house, wrote that his 'worn, pallid look strangely belied the effect of jocularity and high spirits conveyed in his writings. He punned incessantly, but languidly, almost as if unable to think in any other way than a play on words. His smile was attractively sweet: it bespoke the affectionate natured man which his serious verses – those especially addressed to his wife and children – show him to be, and it also revealed the depth of pathos in his soul that inspired his *Bridge of Sighs, Song of the Shirt* and *Eugene Aram*.'

The year 1844 began on a note of optimism and enthusiasm and ushered in the publication of *Hood's Monthly Magazine and Comic Miscellany*, which sold 1500 copies at the first issue, then considered a large circulation for a periodical. The Hoods grew tired of lodgings, having not had a house of their own for eight years, and now they began looking for a home reasonably near to Hood's new offices at 1, Adam Street, Adelphi. They found a property in the New Finchley Road, not far from their old lodgings in St John's Wood and in honour of his former patron, Hood named the house Devonshire Lodge. The magazine flourished under Hood's able editing, with a body of contributors which included Richard Monckton Milnes (later Lord Houghton), Charles Dickens, Sir Edward Bulwer-Lytton and Robert Browning. Another contributor was Samuel Phillips, whose wife had just died. Hood wrote him a note of condolence that reveals something of the patient stoic philosophy that he had formulated during years of his own suffering and disillusion:

> The only comfort I can offer to you is the one which I have found most consolatory under the loss of dear relatives, the belief that we do not love in vain; that so surely as we must live, having lived, so must we love, having loved; and that after some term, longer or shorter, but a mere vibration of the great pendulum of eternity, we shall be reunited. In the meantime let us endure as bravely as we can for the sake of others....I would earnestly recommend you, from my experience, to resume your pen. I have had my share of troubles of this world, as well as of the calamities of authors, and have found it to be a very great blessing to be able to carry my thoughts into ideas, from the too strong reality.[84]

Hood's Magazine for January contained one of Hood's most celebrated and least read poems, *The Haunted House*. The Gothic element in his work has been long forgotten, yet in many points it is typical of his genius. His inner belief in 'supernature', concealed within a shell of humour, occasionally succeeded in breaking out, for his nature consisted of a subtle balance of light and shade that came and went in the night and day of his moodiness. When combined, the intensity of his impressions and the minuteness of his perceptions combine to create a brooding on sinister themes. These themes had at times been treated with reverence, but more often possessed a veneer of humour that suggested as he implied, 'the laughter of a hyena'. This conscious playing with life beyond death and jesting with phantoms from the sea in the early ballads implies an inner fear which had its roots in childhood – perhaps in the diabolical face he had once traced on the ceiling, ever gazing down on him. Such experiences were not uncommon at the time.

When Horace Walpole dreamed of 'a gigantic hand in armour' laid upon the banister, the memory remained imprinted on his mind as the raw material for his Gothic romance, *The Castle of Otranto* (1764), a novel to be followed by *The Mysteries of Udolpho* (1794) by Ann Radcliffe and *Frankenstein* (1818) by Mary Shelley. Here was a world of nightmarish fantasy. The haunted, fearful, trembling characters move wide-eyed through dark forests, shrouded mountains and raging seas, stand doomed and shrunken on perilous crags, or lie crouching in pestilential dungeons in terror and apprehension. They stand rooted to the ground, amid spine-tingling groanings and supernatural loomings. The intimate relationship between character and environment made awesome by the introduction of psychic phenomena and morbid psychological detail became almost a form of mysticism. Nature's silence was not that of death and decay, but of imperceptible and sometimes sinister growth, implacable and remorseless.

The supernatural horrors of *Otranto, Udolpho,* and *Frankenstein* gave rise to a new kind of Gothicism that ultimately dissociated itself from mediaevalism and produced novels, short stories and poetry such as James

Hogg's *The Memoirs and Confessions of a Justified Sinner* (1824) and Edgar Allan Poe's *Tales of the Grotesque and Arabesque* (1839). In their endeavour to create intensity of atmosphere, some writers of Gothic literature fell into excesses and absurdities that destroyed the verisimilitude of the narrative, but in poems such as Browning's *Childe Roland to a Dark Tower Came* (1855) , there is a tremendous accumulative force in the gruesome description and remorseless rhythm of the verse; and so it is with *The Haunted House.* Where Browning kept to the formal pattern of the mediaeval setting, Hood drew more from contemporary life around him.

It is clear that Hood's devotion to the Keatsian idiom in his early poetry was essential to his development as a writer of Gothic verse and we should never have enjoyed the richness of his imagination in *The Haunted House* if he had not experimented fancifully with language in *The Plea of the Midsummer Fairies. The Haunted House* is a masterpiece of craftsmanship. In tone and feeling it is reminiscent of *The Dream of Eugene Aram* but, whereas the latter tells of an appalling fact, *The Haunted House*, a poem of nightmarish impressions, is infused with decay and dread. An oppressive, suffocating air hangs over the silent deserted house with its worm-eaten timbers and its insect swarms. The style invites comparison with Tennyson's *Talking Oak* (1837-8). The language is never carried too far and never detracts from the spontaneity of the inspiration. It is vivid, real, and true to life. The sinister rhythm of the stanza, with its shortened fourth line, is curiously dignified and impressive. The detail is brilliantly observed and starkly moving, clothed as it is in unreality. The ballad-like refrain returns like the unhurried strokes of a phantom bell clanging in the night hours.

Hood excels in those poems in which he exercises his vivid imagination and keen observation in the expression of sinister situations of a physical and psychical nature, poems such as *The Haunted House, The Dream of Eugene Aram, The Forge, The Last Man* and the ballads. The sinister held a fascination for him; his imagination was invariably associated with unpleasant or disagreeable phenomena, which are part of the realm of the highly strung or morbidly oversensitive person. Normally excluded from our conscious life, such phenomena reveal themselves in our nightmares, fears and phobias as dread manifestations of evil. Hood would sketch skulls, grinning skeletons, and coffins, as illustrations of the joke of human existence. Even on his deathbed he could, with grim deliberation, sketch himself in a shroud.

Underlying the poems of macabre circumstance and farcical situation, there is an irrepressible inclination towards the sinister, resting as it does just below the surface of the language, yet imperceptibly linked with the realities of the subject matter, and yet never fully revealed. As he puts it: 'The hyena is notoriously a frequenter of graves, a prowler amongst tombs;

117

he is also the only beast that laughs, at least above his breath.' His profound fascination with the morbid and the spectral gloom of spiritualistic ritual haunts his darker world with thoughts of death and crime and madness; with gibbets on lonely moors at the end of the world, suicides of destitute mothers, and murder revealed in the darkened recesses of the conscience.

From these dark thoughts at the centre of his soul, we move out, centrifugally, towards the circumference of experience; we move almost recklessly into a myriad manifestation of daily life, away from the supernatural into the natural, into the whirling world of laughter and love, punning and practical joking, melancholy and mirth, satire and caricature, that form the outer shell of the soul. Hood lived by association and by analogy: it is by the very minuteness of his perception that he translates the morbidity of his inner soul into intelligible terms that become the true expression of a melancholy, humane and tender nature.

In spite of the publication of *Hood's Magazine,* the happiness at Devonshire Lodge was short-lived. The printing of the February issue was endangered by a lack of funds. There was a quarrel with the printer over payment and another had to be found, but he too refused to undertake work for the price Hood could pay, and so yet another had to be engaged. Even he had not the requisite type in stock and was forced to buy special blocks. It is quite clear from the record of his dealings with other publishers, that Hood had not much of a head for business. He was too trusting perhaps and did not examine contracts with care, so that the terms were not always in his favour, or only barely so. The *Magazine* appeared late, and the news of strained relations between Hood and his publisher soon spread to the distant corners of the publishing world.

The situation certainly had a serious effect on Hood's health as John Blackwood, the Edinburgh publisher, makes clear in a letter to a friend early in the year:

> 'I dined on Friday last with Phillips. Thomas Hood was there, a very quiet fellow, evidently in the most miserable health. He is in a dreadful fix with the man who is associated with him in the unhappy magazine, so I daresay it will speedily come to a close. He has applied to Phillips to arbitrate. P. says the other fellow deluded Hood with a notion that he had money; it turns out that he had only £100, which he has never produced, and grabbed the money received at the office as it came in. Do not say anything about this.'

Two months later, in April 1844, *The Workhouse Clock* appeared. Here is the bustling life of the city and the freshness of the country air: the one where work can be found amid filth and disease of overcrowded factories; the other where health and vigour count for nothing if there is no work to be found. This is the perfect pathetic antithesis that Hood had employed in *The Song of the Shirt*, here used to full effect. We see men coming from many parts to find food – but they are no longer men – they are mere shadows of men – stricken with hunger and disease, they are deformed, crippled and deluded. With typical irony, Hood describes the scene as they pass through Bread Street and Poultry in the City of London on their way to the workhouse, watched by factory hands:

> Stirr'd by an overwhelming zeal,
> And social impulse, a terrible throng!
> Leaving shuttle, and needle, and wheel,
> Furnace, and grindstone, spindle, and reel,
> Thread, and yarn, and iron, and steel –
> Yea, rest and the yet untasted meal –
> Gushing, rushing, crushing along,
> A very torrent of Man!
> Urged by the signs of sorrow and wrong,
> Grown at last to a hurricane strong,
> Stop its course who can!
> Stop who can its onward course
> And irresistible moral force;
> O! vain and idle dream!
> For surely as men are all akin,
> Whether of fair or sable skin,
> According to Nature's scheme,
> That Human Movement contains within
> A Blood-Power stronger than Steam.

The emotional tone of these poems is memorable in the subtle integration of word and rhythm and the fine flow of narrative. The style is immediately recognisable as Hood's own that it is not difficult to see how Dickens discovered the identity of the author of *The Song of the Shirt*.[85]

> With fingers weary and worn,
> With eyelids heavy and red,
> A woman sat, in unwomanly rags,
> Plying her needle and thread –
> Stitch! Stitch! Stitch!
> In poverty, hunger, and dirt,
> And still with a voice of dolorous pitch
> She sang the 'Song of the Shirt!'

119

Ebenezer Elliott's *Corn Law Rhymes* (1831), Elizabeth Barrett Browning's *The Cry of the Children* (1843) and Hood's *The Song of the Shirt, The Workhouse Clock, The Lay of the Labourer* and *The Bridge of Sighs* are supreme utterances against the misery, poverty and helplessness of the working classes in 19th century England. They are part of the literature of indignation and despair; the first murmurings of democracy that brought about a new respect for the individual. The louder voices of Carlyle and Dickens reverberated through society; Robert Owen made new advances in industrial techniques and labour conditions; Lord Shaftesbury and Lord Ashley, by the Factory Acts, rooted out iniquities of child labour and unfenced machinery. and established a maximum number of hours to be worked. Then came the Poor Law Amendment Act and the rise of trade unions. Hood's social verse aroused the indignation of thousands to a protest which, though redolent with sentimentality, broke through the barrier of Victorian idealism and prejudice. He had a predilection for such themes. They touched off his inspiration and set his pen vigorously criticising personalities and events of his time with a virtuosity unparalleled in this genre of poetry. His masterly use of rhythm and rhyme, his adoption of the contemporary idiom and his deep understanding of the simple human needs rendered his work immensely popular with the common reader. After his death, when Edward Moxon began publishing Hood's complete poems, they ran into 19 editions in the 20 years between 1846 and 1866. Hood drew from his readers' feelings both varied and violent: tears and laughter, compassion and indignation interchanged incessantly, though in the end the laughter grew hollow. His humanitarian principles involved him in political controversy but Hood was politically independent, even though he regretted the revolutionary tenor of his poems. His political utterances are few, but when they occur they are frank and brief:

> For my part, I say, hang party! There wants to be a true country party to look singly to the good of England – retrench and economise, reduce taxes, and make it possible to live as cheap at home as abroad. There would be patriotism, instead of mere struggle of Ins and Outs for place and pelf[*].

As early as 1833, in the *Preface* to the *Comic Annual*, he pronounced: 'I have seen but thirty-five summers, and with regret to my Constitution, I am strictly Conservative'. His poetry was not the outcome of any political leaning to right or left. It was a natural expression of an increasingly close association between literature and democracy. He does not write of real

---

[*] Pelf – money or wealth, especially if acquired dishonourably.

misfortune with callousness, as some critics have suggested; he concerns himself with translating reality into moving and pathetic terms. When he had shed the early influences of Shakespeare, Keats, and Byron, he revealed in himself what Wordsworth also demanded from a poet: 'something far more deeply interfused' and, with the fullness of his later years, he at last began to speak from his heart in an original and compelling style.

A breakdown came in May, and on the 22nd of the month, Jane wrote to Dr Elliot:

> 'Last night he fretted dreadfully, and at one this morning, was seized so suddenly with short breathing, and fullness of the chest, I thought he could not live….What can be done to relieve his poor mind, which feels cruelly this failure of a work he has laboured at night and day, and which would have been a good property if carried on.'[86]

The next day was Hood's birthday. Dr Elliot gave a party in honour of the occasion, but Hood was too ill to attend. He continued to sketch and write from his bed, though he was warned that another attack might be fatal. The *Magazine* was not forsaken. A contributor, F.O. Ward, came forward and offered his services free. Dickens, Landor and Browning rallied round, the first of whom contributed *A Threatening Letter to Thomas Hood from an Ancient Gentleman*[87] – in part a satire on the current craze for such midgets as Tom Thumb.

A notable contribution to this number was from Hood himself, yet another poem on social distress; it was *The Bridge of Sighs*,[88] a profoundly pathetic poem which aroused public interest in no less degree than *The Song of the Shirt*. It tells of a fallen woman who had drowned herself by leaping from Waterloo Bridge into the River Thames, combining speculation as to the tragically sinful life she might have led with the symbolism of the river cleansing her of her impurities. It was said to have been inspired by the heavily publicised case of Mary Furley, which occurred only a few weeks before the poem was composed; Mary was a poor seamstress who attempted to drown herself and her two young children in The Regent's Canal. She succeeded in drowning one child before she was rescued from the water and arrested; she was sentenced to hang, but a public outcry, aroused by her abject poverty, resulted in a lesser sentence of seven years transportation.

Browning praised it as a poem 'alone in its generation', and indeed it reflects with simplicity and pathos the true spirit of the age:

> One more Unfortunate,
> Weary of breath,
> Rashly importunate,
> Gone to her death!

Take her up tenderly,
Lift her with care;
Fashion'd so slenderly,
Young, and so fair!

Found Drowned by George Frederic Watts RA (1817-1904). 1867. Oil on canvas.
Based on Hood's poem *The Bridge of Sighs* (Watts Gallery, Compton)

Mary Russell Mitford wrote of this poem as 'one gush of tenderness and charity'. Consider this treatment of the moment when the young girl stands on the bridge before she plunges to her death:

Where the lamps quiver
So far in the river,
With many a light
From window and casement,
From garret to basement,
She stood, with amazement,
Houseless by night.

The bleak wind of March
Made her tremble and shiver;
But not the dark arch,
Or the black flowing river:
Mad from life's history,
Glad to death's mystery,
Swift to be hurl'd –

Anywhere, anywhere,
Out of the world!

In July 1844, a slight recovery enabled Hood to convalesce for two months at Vanbrugh House, Blackheath, 'that goose-pie of a castle, built on the model of the Bastille, which Vanbrugh built for himself on the Park side of the Heath'.[89] He wrote to Phillips of a projected day trip to Calais with Fanny and of having his bust modelled: 'My bust is modelled and cast. It is said to be a correct likeness; two parts Methodist, to one of Humourist, and quite recognisable in spite of the Hood all over the face.' Assessing his position he goes on: 'We are very poor and have only seventy-two thousand a year (pence mind, not pounds), and our names not even in the Post Office Directory, much less the Court Guide!'[90]

It was thought that the clay soil of the neighbourhood of Devonshire Lodge did not agree with him, and that they should move yet again to London for the winter, so that he could be nearer his doctor. 'Indeed I am sorry to say he is never well now,' Jane wrote in a letter to de Franck, 'unable to walk the shortest distance without suffering, and feeling every change of weather.'[91] To this letter, Hood added a cheerful little postscript: 'Three doctors could not kill me, so I *may* live a year or two.' In the event, the move did not take place, and Dr Elliot travelled 10 miles every day to visit Hood during this critical stage of his sickness.

The November number of the *Magazine* contained Hood's *The Lay of the Labourer*. Like its predecessors, it is a powerful denunciation of a social injustice, and points out the desperate need for reform in the agricultural community, hitherto the province of Cobbett and Ebenezer Elliott. Whilst Elliott, whose work Carlyle claimed as 'hues of joy and harmony painted out of troublous tears', was concerned with ideas of cheap bread and the anti-capitalist movement, Cobbett had a wider appeal and a more substantial remedy. Life for him was meant to be lived with honesty and temperance in a world free from 'insufficiency' of food and raiment. Hard work, good health, 'plentiful food, sweet air and abundant exercise' were essential to the self-respect of the labourer. In such a world, the diligent and honest man could disdain the 'insolence of riches', breathe in the morning air, refute the concept that poverty is noble, and experience 'the strongest of all feelings – the love of life'. Cobbett's visit to North America had shown him that hard work and frugality were the basis of a stable society; that 'big barns and modest dwelling houses' were preferable to pauperism and the workhouse. His warning that 'from endeavouring to imitate perfection men arrive at mediocrity' went unheeded. The factory worker and agricultural labourer became unwilling and helpless victims of the great experiment in which inventors, industrialists, politicians and investors were engaged.

Hood had his own views on progress and its effects on the lower classes, but unlike Cobbett and Elliott, who had their own special axes to grind, Hood was far more influenced by personal distress. The emotional aspects of injustice touched the strings of his sensibility. and brought forth some of his best writing, including his most inspired and convincing poetry. In the spring of 1844, an 18-year-old labourer was sentenced to transportation to the colonies for life for sending a threatening letter to local Huntingdonshire farmers saying that, if he did not find work soon, he would set fire to their farm buildings. Hood cut the account of the case out of his newspaper and placed it on his mantleshelf, referring to it constantly and pondering on the predicament of the young boy. *The Lay of the Labourer* was a plea to the public conscience to alleviate the suffering of the starving unemployed.[92] In particular, it was addressed to the Home Secretary, to whom a copy was forwarded. The Minister replied briefly and noncommittally: 'Sir James Graham presents his compliments to Mr. Hood, and begs to acknowledge *The Magazine* accompanying his letter of the 30th instant.' Such a reply did not surprise Hood. He had scarcely hoped to impress him: 'I fear he will do no more; they say he is a cold, hard man bigoted to the New Poor Law.'

Hood had a profound compassion for those who suffered from poverty, which he regarded as the degradation of human dignity. The rapidly increasing wealth of the country had done nothing to relieve conditions of the poor. The domestic system still survived in the textile industry as a legacy from pre-industrial revolution days. Now it was almost unworkable compared with the efficiency of mass production, and for those who continued to spin at home, wages were pitifully low and destitution lay just round the corner.

Greater objectivity is achieved by travelling abroad and seeing society from afar, and both Byron and Hood were strengthened by exile. Cobbett, on his return from America, had taken up the cause of the agricultural labourer, while Hood turned to the individual tragedies that lay unnoticed below the routine existence of daily life. Both men saw that improvement in the standard of living of the poorer classes was dependent on better conditions of work and higher wages; by this means alone could the self-respect of the working man be restored. It was a challenge soon to be taken up by periodicals and newspapers. *Punch*, with its overtly humanitarian principles, sought to criticise religion, politics, education and social evils under the cloak of caricature. The shadow of Blake's 'dark Satanic Mills' loomed over the Pennines as a testimony to man's inhumanity to man, whilst, in London, a sensational story like that of the seamstress did much to bring the problem into the open.

The Song of The Shirt sparked off new enthusiasms for philanthropic gestures. Hood hoped the poem would leave an indelible scar on the public conscience. Though he had written far better things, the poem had more effect than anything else he had published. The new rich quaked as their conscience smarted at this vivid and outspoken criticism. In their effort to march in step with the progress and idealism of the times, they had inadvertently overlooked the fact that such idealism had begun with charity and compassion. In *The Lady's Dream*,[93] a contrast is drawn between the luxury and ease of a lady's past life and her dream – a vision of the poor and hungry. The lady of some wealth lies on her 'couch so soft and warm', unable to sleep. At last she succeeds, only to have a nightmare that fills her with horror and remorse, for her dream is one of human misery. She is shown, like Scrooge, the sufferings of the poor, dying in their thousands in a 'World of Woe', a hell of hunger and disease, peopled by the crippled, the blind, the helpless, and the starving. Her remorse is measureless:

> 'I drank the richest draughts;
>   And ate whatever is good –
> Fish, and flesh, and fowl, and fruit
>   Supplied my hungry mood;
> But never remembered the wretched ones
>   That starve for want of food!
>
> 'I dress'd as the noble dress,
>   In cloth of silver and gold,
> With silk, and satin, and costly furs,
>   In many an ample fold;
> But I never remembered the naked limb
>   That froze with winter's cold.
>
> The wounds I might have heal'd!
>   The human sorrow and smart!
> And yet it never was in my soul
>   To play so ill a part:
> But evil is wrought by want of Thought,
>   As well as want of Heart!
>
> She clasp'd her fervent hands,
>   And the tears began to stream;
> Large, and bitter, and fast they fell,
>   Remorse was so extreme:
> And yet, oh yet, that many a Dame
>   Would dream the Lady's dream!

Aware of the serious state of Hood's health, several of his friends decided to place his claims, as a literary man, before the government, as grounds for the grant of a pension. Not only would the future of his close family be secured in the event of his death, but he would be spared the anxieties and harassing exertions to which he was continually subjected. Towards the end of 1844, the project had gathered support from the likes of the Earl of Ellesmere, Lord Wharncliffe and Richard Monkton Milnes. Hood received a semi-official notice requesting him to name a close female relative on whom a pension might be conferred, as his own life was so precarious. Hood named his wife, and wrote to the Prime Minister, Sir Robert Peel:

> 'As an Author I cannot but think it a good omen for the cause, that this mark of your favour has fallen on a writer so totally unconnected with party politics as myself, whose favourite theory of Government is "An Angel from Heaven, and a Despotism."
> As a Man, I am deeply sensible of a consideration and kindness, which have made this "work-a-day" world more park-like to me… and will render the poor remnant of my life much happier, and easier, than it could be with the prospect that was before me.'[94]

On Hood's return from Brighton six days later, Peel sent an official communication by special messenger that the Queen had confirmed that an annuity of £100 should be conferred on Jane Hood for the remainder of her life. Peel's letters to Hood give sufficient proof that Hood's work had not gone unnoticed in political circles.

THE SONG OF THE SHIRT

With fingers weary and worn,
  With eyelids heavy and red,
A woman sat in unwomanly rags,
  Plying her needle and thread—
    Stitch! stitch! stitch!
In poverty, hunger, and dirt,
  And still with a voice of dolorous pitch
She sang the "Song of the Shirt."

  "Work! work! work!
While the cock is crowing aloof!
  And work—work—work,
Till the stars shine through the roof!
It's O! to be a slave
  Along with the barbarous Turk,
Where woman has never a soul to save,
  If this is Christian work!

  "Work—work—work,
Till the brain begins to swim;
  Work—work—work,
Till the eyes are heavy and dim!
Seam, and gusset, and band,
  Band, and gusset, and seam,
Till over the buttons I fall asleep,
  And sew them on in a dream!

  "O, men, with sisters dear!
  O, men, with mothers and wives!
It is not linen you're wearing out,
  But human creatures' lives!
    Stitch—stitch—stitch,
  In poverty, hunger and dirt,
Sewing at once, with a double thread,
  A Shroud as well as a Shirt.

"But why do I talk of death?
    That phantom of grisly bone,
I hardly fear his terrible shape,
    It seems so like my own—
It seems so like my own,
    Because of the fasts I keep;
Oh, God! that bread should be so dear.
    And flesh and blood so cheap!

"Work—work—work!
    My labour never flags;
And what are its wages? A bed of straw,
    A crust of bread—and rags.
That shattered roof—this naked floor—
    A table—a broken chair—
And a wall so blank, my shadow I thank
    For sometimes falling there!

"Work—work—work!
    From weary chime to chime,
Work—work—work,
    As prisoners work for crime!
Band, and gusset, and seam,
    Seam, and gusset, and band,
Till the heart is sick, and the brain benumbed,
    As well as the weary hand.

"Work—work—work,
In the dull December light,
    And work—work—work,
When the weather is warm and bright—
While underneath the eaves
    The brooding swallows cling
As if to show me their sunny backs
    And twit me with the spring.

"O! but to breathe the breath
Of the cowslip and primrose sweet—
   With the sky above my head,
And the grass beneath my feet;
For only one short hour
   To feel as I used to feel,
Before I knew the woes of want
   And the walk that costs a meal!

"O! but for one short hour!
   A respite however brief!
No blessed leisure for Love or hope,
   But only time for grief!
A little weeping would ease my heart,
   But in their briny bed
My tears must stop, for every drop
   Hinders needle and thread!"

"Seam, and gusset, and band,
 Band, and gusset, and seam,
     Work, work, work,
 Like the Engine that works by Steam!
 A mere machine of iron and wood
   That toils for Mammon's sake—
 Without a brain to ponder and craze
   Or a heart to feel—and break!"

With fingers weary and worn,
   With eyelids heavy and red,
A woman sat in unwomanly rags,
   Plying her needle and thread—
     Stitch! stitch! stitch!
   In poverty, hunger, and dirt,
And still with a voice of dolorous pitch,—
Would that its tone could reach the Rich!—
   She sang this "Song of the Shirt!"

Chapter 13 - Farewell, Life!

It was now evident to his friends and family that Hood was slowly declining in strength and had not long to live. He continued to write, as a letter to Dr Elliott shows: 'My well is not yet dry. I have pumped out a sheet already of Christmas fun, am drawing some cuts, and shall write a sheet more of my novel.'[95] This was his unfinished novel *Our Family,* eventually published in 1861. His creative will was strong enough to overcome his physical malaise and mould it to his irrepressible humour: 'To make laugh is my calling; I must jump, I must grin, I must tumble, I must turn language head over heels, and leap through grammar.' Lying in bed he must have seemed like a Grimaldi without grease paint. The fusion of inner melancholy and verbal clowning converted him into a literary Pagliaccio[*]. Pathetic now, lovable, sympathetic to the troubles of others, ignoring his grave condition, he continued working, occasionally propped up in an easy chair, writing letters such as this one to Thackeray on 4th August 1844:

> My dear Thackeray, − I am grieved to hear of your ill health, and sincerely trust that before many days intervene you will have thoroughly recovered. I fear that so far as I myself am concerned King Death will claim me ere many months elapse. However, there's a good time coming, if not in this world, most assuredly in the next. Always yours, − Thos. Hood.

Thackeray in his turn reminisced on Hood's courage and tenacity:

> What he has to do he does with all his might, through sickness, through sorrow, through exile, poverty, fever, depression, there he is, always ready to his work, and with a jewel of genius in his pocket. Why when he laid down his puns and pranks, put the motley off, and spoke out of his heart, all England and America listened with tears and wonder! ....Oh, sad, marvellous picture of courage, of honesty, of patient endurance, of duty struggling against pain. How noble Peel's figure is, standing by that sick bed! How generous his words, how dignified and sincere his compassion!

---

[*] Pagliaccio – Italian for clown, vis. *Pagliacci* (clowns) opera by Leoncavallo

The Prime Minister had shown his devotion to Hood both in deed and word, having been responsible for the Queen conferring the life pension on Jane Hood and by writing the celebrated letter of confirmation, which Hood so gratefully received on his deathbed:

> You perhaps think that you are known to one with such multifarious duties as myself, merely by general reputation as an author; but I assure you that there can be little which you have written and acknowledged, which I have not read; and that there are few who can appreciate and admire more than myself, the good sense and good feeling which have taught you to infuse so much fun and merriment into writings correcting folly and exposing absurdities, and yet never trespassing beyond those limits within which wit and facetiousness are not very often combined.

In this assessment of Hood's status as a poet, Peel was expressing the view of many thousands of people who had admired the constant flow of ingenuity that Hood had maintained for over 20 years. His life is a testimony to the meticulousness and feelings with which he imbued his work. He never once considered writing poetry as a pleasant pastime. Even when he turned to engraving as a career he was trying hard to establish his position as a creative artist and to discover his true potentialities. A wistful note creeps into his words sometimes, as he writes in the preface to *Hood's Own*:

> I seem to have retained my shadow and sold my substance. In short, as happens to prematurely old port wine, I am of a bad colour with very little body. But what then? That emaciated hand still lends a hand to embody in words and sketches, the creations or recreations of a Merry Fancy: those gaunt sides shake heartily as ever at the Grotesques and Arabesques and droll Picturesques that my Good Genius (a Pantagruelian* Familiar) charitably conjures up to divert me from more sombre realities.

In 1830 he had written that it was his humble hope and aim to contribute towards the laughter and lustiness of his fellow creatures: an early hint of the Pantagruelian Familiar. A man as widely read as Hood could not fail to

---

* Pantegruelian – huge, enormous, gigantic. Pantagruel was the huge son of Gargantua in *Pantagruel* by the French author François Rabelais.

see his affinities with a writer like Rabelais, whose optimism, hope, courage, inventiveness, humanity and lust for life were uppermost in his work. Both excelled in their astonishing command of words, in their multitudinous manifestations of verbal ingenuity, their hatred of hypocrisy, and the narrow asceticism and gloom that covered the religion of their times. It seems that, with the disappointment of his 1827 volume, *Whims and Oddities*, Hood was reconciled to the fact that his destiny lay in the direction of humour. A few years later, in the second edition of *Copyright and Copywrong,* he refused to succumb to self-pity; rather did he maintain his self-respect in spite of frustrated ambition: 'I am far from therefore considering myself as an overlooked, under-kept, wet blanket, hid-under-the-bushel, or lapped-in-a-napkin individual.' As the years passed, in periods of sickness punctuated by brief moments of happiness in the family circle, he developed a stoic philosophy, displaying great fortitude in the face of his physical afflictions.

In Canon Ainger's words, Hood possessed 'a constitutional attraction towards the tragedies of life'. Out of these tragedies, projected as they were through the spectrum of his own complexity and suffering, he drew a vision of man at once vivid and true, enhanced as he grew older by the generosity and humanity that surged in his soul. He oscillated between extremes of comic and Gothic, fanciful and didactic, until the various parts of his personality fused at last into a single expression of hope and charity that filled the hearts of those who knew him, and read his last humanitarian appeals. He never forgot that laughter was the great antidote for poverty, pain, suffering, hunger and misery; neither did he forget that laughter is the most subtle means of driving home a vital point of criticism. Writing of himself in *A Portrait,* he says:

> Who, that calls himself a stranger, could ever suppose that such a pale, pensive, peaking, sentimental, sonneteering countenance – with a wry mouth as if it always laughing on its wrong side – belonged bona fide to the Editor of the Comic – a Professor of the Pantagruelian Philosophy?....I do not mind telling my face to its face that it insinuates a false Hood, and grossly misrepresents a person notorious amongst friends for laughing at strange times and odd places, and in particular when he has the worst of the rubber.

Such statements are to be found throughout the whole of his work. Hood provides a rational and objective analysis of his situation, advising his readers thus: '....I never meet trouble half way, but let him have the whole walk for his pains', but he stoically reminds them of his own plight:

'…misfortunes with me never came singly, from my very childhood…I am born to suffer, whether done by accident or done by design.' Weak in body he may have been, but he had a toughness of constitution that resisted all death's attempts to end it. Writing in the preface to *Hood's Own* while he was in Germany he explained his system of Practical Cheerful Philosophy:

> I have converted a serious illness into a comic wellness. By what other agency could I have transported myself, as a Cockney would say, from *Dull*age to *Grin*age [Dulwich to Greenwich]. It was far from a practical joke to be laid up in ordinary in a foreign land, under the Physicians quite as much abroad as myself with the case; indeed the shades of the gloaming were stealing over my prospects; but I resolved that, like the sun, so long as my day lasted, I would look on the bright side of everything. The raven croaked, but I persuaded myself that it was the nightingale; there was the smell of the mould, but I remembered that it nourished the violets.

Dickens, writing to Angela Burdett-Coutts from Rome on 18 March, expressed his concern for Hood's condition:

> …I also hear privately that Hood, the author, is past all chance of recovery. He was (I have a presentiment that even now I may speak of him as something past) a man of great power – of prodigious force and genius as a poet – and not generally known, perhaps, by his best credentials. Personally, he had a most noble and generous spirit…so free from any taint of envy or reluctance to acknowledge me as a young man far more fortunate than himself, that I can hardly bear to think of it.

By the early spring of 1845 Hood knew that it might be only a matter of weeks before the end came. He set himself to writing farewell letters to his closest friends, many of whom visited him: friends such as F.O. Ward, the voluntary unpaid editor of *Hood's Monthly Magazine*, who described the scene thus: 'He saw the oncoming of death with great cheerfulness, though without anything approaching levity;…He conversed for about an hour in his old playful way, with now and then a word or two of deep and tender feelings. When I left he bade me goodbye, and kissed me, shedding tears, and saying that perhaps we never should meet again.' On 1st April, the *Magazine* announced his approaching death thus:

His sufferings, which have lately undergone a terrible increase, have been throughout sustained with manly fortitude and Christian resignation. He is perfectly aware of his condition; and we have no longer any reason, or any right to speak ambiguously of a now too certain loss, the loss of a Great Writer – great in the splendour of his copious imagery, in his rare faculty of terse incisive language, in his power and pregnancy of thought, – and in his almost Shakespearean versatility of genius, great in the few, but noble works he leaves behind, greater still perhaps, in those he will carry unwritten to his early tomb.[96]

Friends and strangers rallied round him, one anonymously sending £20 and a note saying: 'A Shirt! And a sincere wish for health'. Another sent verses *'To T. Hood, on Hearing of His Sickness'*. It was probably at this time that he wrote his last poem, *Stanzas*:

> Farewell, Life! My senses swim;
> And the world is growing dim;
> Thronging shadows cloud the light,
> Like the advent of the night, –
> Colder, colder, colder still
> Upward steals a vapour chill –
> Strong the earthy odour grows –
> I smell the Mould above the Rose!
>
> Welcome Life! The spirit strives!
> Strength returns, and hope revives;
> Cloudy fears and shapes forlorn
> Fly like shadows at the morn, –
> O'er the earth there comes a bloom –
> Sunny light for sullen gloom,
> Warm perfume for vapour cold –
> I smell the Rose above the Mould!

It was a beautiful spring. Hood lay looking out of his window at the newness of nature as it flowed and flourished. 'It's a beautiful world,' he remarked, 'and since I have been lying here, I have thought of it more and more; it is not so bad, even humanly speaking, as people would make out. I have had some very happy days while I lived in it, and I could have wished to stay a little longer. But it is all for the best, and we shall all meet in a better world!' He fell into a delirium soon after but regained consciousness enough to call his family to him. To his wife he said: 'Remember, Jane, I

134

forgive all, <u>all</u>, as I hope to be forgiven.' She bending over him, heard him whisper 'O Lord! Say, Arise take up thy cross, and follow me!' Soon, he sank into the sleep of death and after 36 hours he died. It was midday on 3rd May 1845, just three weeks before his 46th birthday.

Chapter 14 – Hood's Legacy

Just as Thomas Hood senior had left his family impoverished at his death in 1811, now Hood, the poet, was to leave his family behind him to face a life of destitution. Jane Hood inherited nothing but debts, a situation which soon subjected her affairs to the scrutiny of a public appeal. The fund was launched by Hood's faithful editor, Frederick Oldfield Ward, who had valiantly carried through the press the final numbers of *Hood's Magazine*, and the indefatigable friend and admirer, Richard Monckton Milnes (later Lord Houghton). This was with the support of the Prime Minister, Sir Robert Peel, William Harvey (the distinguished engraver of the illustrations to *The Dream of Eugene Aram*), Thomas Carlyle, and others. Dickens, however, felt that the appeal was weakened by the existence of a pension which had been granted to Hood's dependents from monies made available by the Queen from the Privy Purse, and it was dropped. Jane and her two children were now left without adequate means of subsistence. In addition, the suggestion that Hood should be buried in Poets' Corner at Westminster Abbey, in the company of Spenser, Dryden and Jonson, had also to be abandoned for lack of the necessary £200 fee required by the Abbey authority.

Hood was buried in the new cemetery at Kensal Green on 10 May 1845. His funeral was a private and quiet affair, though attended by many who had known and loved him. Sir Robert Peel would have attended, but was prevented by a pre-existing public engagement. Tom Hood recollects that it was a beautiful spring day, and just as the service ended a lark rose up, mounting and singing over the heads of the mourners.[97] Jane, worn out by the constant anxieties of Hood's final illness, was soon to follow him there, for she died in December 1846.

Thus Fanny, now sixteen years of age, and Tom, eleven, were left to grieve the loss of both their parents, in a financial situation that was little short of destitution. There was not even enough money to buy their departed parents a tombstone, and Hood's grave remained untended for several years.

It was not until 1854, after yet another appeal for funds, that a monument was eventually unveiled at Kensal Green, with the support of Hood's kindly patron, the Duke of Devonshire. Thomas De Quincey, whom Hood had known since the days as sub-editor of the *London Magazine*, and Mary Russell Mitford, the author of *Our Village*, on which Hood had based his humorous monologue of the same name, also supported the appeal. Other contributors included Longfellow, Macaulay, and not least the popular poetess and organiser of the appeal, Eliza Cook, whose verses in *Punch* had helped to bring the matter to the notice of the public:

> Give him the dust beneath his head,
> Give him a grave – a grave alone –
> In Life he dearly won his bread; –
> In Death he was not worth a stone.

Those words were powerful enough to set the appeal in motion and subscriptions flowed in from Members of Parliament, men of letters, and people from all sections of society. One came from Longfellow, who had not forgotten his visit to the Hoods years before: 'Poor Mrs. Hood and the children, who have lost him! They will have forgotten the stranger who called one October morning, with Dickens, and was hospitably entertained by them. But I remember the visit, and the pale face of a poet, and the house in St. John's Wood.' Longfellow was not to know then that Jane Hood too had followed her husband into death.

On 18 July 1854, Richard Monckton Milnes delivered a graveside oration in praise of Hood, speaking movingly of Hood's contribution to the literature of his country. Standing nearby, among many friends and admirers, were humble men and women who had come to do honour to their poet and to read the simple epitaph:

'He Sang the Song of the Shirt.'

Hood's design for his tombstone

The monument, surmounted by a bust, and flanked by oval *bas reliefs* depicting scenes from *The Dream of Eugene Aram* and *The Bridge of Sighs*, is today a poignant reminder of the vanity of human wishes, for the bust of Hood has been stolen, the *bas reliefs* have been prised from their place by vandals, leaving only gaping grey ovals of rough stone to trouble the eye of visiting 'pilgrims':

"Poor Hood!" for whom a people wreaths
  The heart-born flowers that never die.
"Poor Hood!" for whom a requiem breathes
  In every human Toil-wrung sigh.

And let thy Soul serenely sleep
  While pilgrims stand as I have stood;
To worship at a nameless heap,
  And fondly, sadly say, "Poor Hood!"

The tombstone of Thomas Hood in Kensal Green cemetery

The neglected appearance of Hood's grave is today sadly symptomatic of the decline and fall of both man and poet. The story of his life is a salutary lesson to all those individuals, whether poets or not, who, out of idealism or ill-founded optimism, believe that charity dwells with vested interests and the established order of things rather than in the home. Hood was attacked for his unfashionable libertarian views, for his free-thinking Christianity, and his refusal to subscribe to Party. In writing to his sub-editor, Frederick Oldfield Ward, in July 1845, Hood listed a number of precepts by which he had lived out his life. Among them were:

> …I may be said to have favoured liberal principles; but then they were so liberal as to be *catholic*…
>
> I have not devoted any comic power I may possess to lays of indecency or ribaldry…
>
> I have never written against religion: any Pseudo Saints & Pharisees, notwithstanding…
>
> I have never been indicted for libel.
>
> I have never been called out for personality [personal abuse].
>
> I have not sought pleasure or profit in satirising or running down my literary contemporaries.
>
> I have never stolen from them.
>
> I have never written *anonymously* what I should object to own.
>
> I have never countenanced, by my practice, the puffery, quackery & trickery of modern literature – even when publishing for years on my own account. In short, though I may not have reflected any great honour on our national literature, I have not disgraced it. All of which has been an infinite comfort to me to remember…
>
> Personally – I am not very sensitive on the score of poverty since it has been the lot of many of those whose names I most do venerate. The reproach clings not to them but to the country they helped to glorify: My debts & difficulties indeed cost me trouble and concern: but much less than if they had been the result of stark extravagance or vicious dissipation. At the very worst, like Timon, 'unwisely not ignobly have I spent', – & even that to a small amount. But like Dogberry, I have had losses – & been weighed down by drawbacks I should long ago have surmounted but for the continued misconduct and treacheries of others: – called friends and relations. Only, it provokes and vexes me that my position countenances the old traditional twaddle about the improvidence &c. of authors, want of business habits, ignorance of the world &c &c. Men can hardly be ignorant, in particular of what they professedly study – as to business, authors know their own, as well as your mercantiles or traders, & perhaps something

of accounts besides. That they do not thrive like those who seek for money & nothing else is a matter of course: nor can they be expected to prove a match for those whose life-long study has been how to over-reach or swindle. Their Flights have been in another direction. Their contemplations, turned towards the beautiful the just & the good. They are not simple spooney victims – but martyrs to their own code. To cope with the Baillys, & Flights, one must be not merely literary men, but literary scamps – rogues – sharpers. Authors are supposed too often to be mere ninnies, and therefore plucked, especially: in wit men, but in simplicity mere children. A vulgar errour... I have entered into this matter, partly because it may seem that with my popularity I ought to have done better, – & partly because I am jealous of the honour of Authorship...

It is manifest from this defence of his position that Hood had been in desperate straits in the months before his death. Confined to bed by mortal illness, deserted by relations, sickened by the defection of friends, beaten by the 'puffery, quackery & trickery' of the less worthy part of the publishing fraternity with whom he had done business, a man reduced to abject poverty, a poet at once admired and neglected by those who were in a position to help, he had, on the point of death, to find the strength and will to justify his life, all for the sake of a meagre pension. His 'liberal principles' had not been as popular with those in authority as he might have wished. It was true that he never flinched from speaking out on touchy political and social issues when he found it necessary to do so, but he invariably chose to fight his battles on quicksand, without hope of ever being pulled free. His courage and determination to succeed where others had failed can only leave us with feelings of admiration.

Hood was in no way a revolutionary, though some considered him radical enough, in his wish to remain aloof from the politics of Party. He was a man of feeling and hence of compassion. His work is softened by the warmth of his personal philosophy, his love of family, his respect for his fellow man. Like Tennyson's Ulysees, his hardships and endeavours had led him to the belief that the sum purpose of life was 'to strive, to seek, to find, and not to yield.' In that belief he was a true Victorian. He had come far from his romantic roots, yet it was those very roots that that had nurtured his social conscience and compassion, and were the mainspring for his most vibrant and passionate poetical achievements. His resilience in times of anguish and hardship is only to be wondered at. Like Browning, he was:

One who never turned his back but marched breast forward,
  Never doubted clouds would break,
Never dreamed, though right were worsted, wrong would triumph,
  Held we fall to rise, are baffled to fight better,
Sleep to wake.[*]

The reasons for the decline and fall of Thomas Hood are not easy to establish. They become clearer if we trace the path of his reputation in the hundred years following his death in 1845. It seems that he was no exception to the rule that governs the fortunes of great men immediately following their deaths – a rapid rise to popularity, then oblivion. Reputations are invariably the victims of fashion, subject to the caprices of the passing years, surviving only with difficulty the changes and eccentricities of manners and mores. Hood's works were commonly subjected to critical judgements which preferred to recognise only his comic genius. When whimsical, punning kind of humour was not quite the thing, there was little that remained by which to remember him. Shakespeare puts into the mouth of discredited Cardinal Wolsey words which would not have been out of place in soliloquy by the dying Thomas Hood:

Farewell! a long farewell to all my greatness!
This is the state of man: to-day he puts forth
The tender leaves of hopes, to-morrow blossoms,
And bears his blushing honours thick upon him:
The third day comes a frost, a killing frost,
And, - when he thinks, good easy man, full surely
His greatness is a-ripening, - nips his root,
And then he falls, as I do...[†]

A number of distinguished critics have helped to establish the pattern of Hood criticism, beginning with David Masson's essay, written after the publication in 1860 of *The Memorials of Thomas Hood*, a collection of letters and family papers with reminiscences by his son, Tom Hood, and his daughter, Frances Freeling Broderip. The *Memorials* attempted to give a coherent account of Hood's life and work, though they contained very little that is useful in the way of a critical assessment of the poems. From then

---

[*] from Robert Browning - *Epilogue*
[†] Wolsey's Farewell to His Greatness, from Act III, Scene 2, of Shakespeare's *Henry VIII*

on, publishers enthusiastic enough to carry the torch of fame on Hood's behalf were not idle in keeping his name alive.

For thirty years, the firm of a devoted friend, Edward Moxon (succeeded by his son in 1858) kept his popular editions of Hood's works before the public, reissuing *Whims and Oddities* (1854), *Up the Rhine* (1869) and *Hood's Own* (1873), whilst in America, Epes Sargent's edition (1854) and that of Richard Monckton Milnes (1859) were the most successful. Apart from the monumental *Complete Works*, edited by Tom and Frances in 1862-1863, which formed the basis for all other editions for the rest of the century, other editors included William Michael Rossetti, whose splendid *de luxe* edition was illustrated by Gustave Doré, Canon Alfred Ainger (1893), a perceptive critic of Hood's work, and Richard Herne Sheppard (1897, reprinted 1906).

After 1876, the name of Moxon & Son disappears from the title pages and the publication was carried on variously by Ward Lock, Frederick Warne, Routledge, and Chatto and Windus, until the Oxford University Press took on the task in 1906 with Walter Jerrold's *Complete Poetical Works of Thomas Hood* (reprinted 1911). No work had done so much for Hood's reputation since the *Complete Works* on 1862-3. Jerrold went back to original manuscripts where he could, corrected errors of transcription, established punctuation and alignment, and generally prepared for the press the most reliable annotated edition at that time. It is the Jerrold edition that is (or was) to be more commonly found on the shelves of public libraries and second-hand bookshops.

The fashion for drawing-room songs and ballads led many Victorian composers to search for suitable poetry, following the popular success of Thomas Anderton's setting of *I Remember* in the 1820s. By the 1860s and 1870s, many composers were looking to Hood for inspiration. His earlier works provided the kind of texture they looked for – succinctly expressed verses with simple rhyming patterns. He has 'a peculiar kind of voice that speaks from the heart.' Typical of these songs were Charles Gounod's 'There is dew for the flow'ret/And honey for the bee', and Hubert Parry's setting of 'Autumn' –'The Autumn skies are flush'd with gold/ and fair and bright the rivers run.' Gustav Holst's 'I love thee', Peter Warlock's 'A lake and a fairy boat', Granville Bantock's 'The silken thread', Roger Quilter's 'The time of roses', Coleridge-Taylor's 'The lee shore', and Montague Phillips's 'The stars are with the voyager' are only a few of the countless settings of Hood's poetry to be found in the British Library collections. Gounod, immensely successful in Britain, and his fellow composers, in addition to their literary contemporaries, contributed to the survival of Hood's reputation, at least until after the first World War, when society had the wish to 'ring out the old and ring in the new', just as Tennyson had predicted in *In Memoriam.*

The present author has himself composed a number of settings of Hood's poems, including 'Autumn', 'The Stars are with the Voyager', 'The Exile', and 'Still Glides the Gentle Streamlet'.

Apart from Jerrold's edition, Hood's poems fared worse in the twentieth century than in the nineteenth, when Moxon held the monopoly with the edition edited by Hood's son and daughter, a work readily available to the common reader. Apart from Sir Francis Burnand's edition (1907), I have traced only one edition from the inter-war years, that of Hannaford Burnett (1924). It is clear that Hood's reputation was at its nadir. In 1914, the old Victorian social and moral values were seriously challenged, and authors like Hood went to the wall. The times were far too serious for his 'puns and pranks', as Thackeray called them. In 1939, public librarians were asked to throw out all their unread authors to help the salvage campaign for waste paper, as a means of helping the war effort. Hood was among them. No-one read him, and he was pulped down with the rest. After the war was over, Clifford Dyment filled the gap with his brief selection (1948), which once more restored to life *The Dream of Eugene Aram, Fair Ines, Ruth, The Elm Tree, The Bridge of Sighs*, and *The Song of the Shirt*. In 1963, the present author edited the first critical anthology of Hood's poetry and prose, illustrated with his woodcuts, but the timing was not right for a revival, and publishers would not commit themselves. It seemed that the ghost of Thomas Hood, which had so recently made its reappearance, had been laid at last. A recession in the publishing trade was no time to revive a literary corpse. As Hood constantly reminds us, in his verses and woodcuts, skeletons, whether literary or not, make uncomfortable companions.

> O William dear! O William dear!
>   My rest eternal ceases;
> Alas! my everlasting peace
>   Is broken into peaces.
>
> The body-snatchers they have come,
>   And made a snatch at me;
> It's very hard them kind of men
>   Won't let a body be!
>
> Don't go and weep upon my grave,
>   And think that there I be;
> They haven't left an atom there
>   Of my anatomie.

The impression we have of Hood's poetry today remains confused and distorted, despite an abundance of criticism in the form of memoirs, essays, articles and reviews to draw on. Most of this criticism, however, is available to us only in research libraries. Two more recent selections of Hood's poems have failed to catch the public imagination or alter the general opinion that Hood is little more than a maker of punning ballads and faintly amusing domestic verses. He is, in respect of his so-called 'serious' poetry, reduced in the minds of many readers to the lowly ranks of poetaster. Hardly a publisher is prepared to take up the challenge and enter the lists on Hood's behalf, notwithstanding the favourable opinions of past and present critics and biographers. Walter Jerrold, Edmund Blunden, V.S. Pritchett, Laurence Brander, Leslie Marchand, Alvin Whitley, J.M. Cohen, J.C. Reid, and others, have all contributed in their own way to our knowledge of Hood, both man and poet.

Neglected in his native land, his cause has been taken up on other shores. John Clubbe's study of Hood's later career, *Victorian Forerunner* (1968), and *Selected Poems of Thomas Hood* (1970), helped to revive Hood's name across the Atlantic, much as Epes Sargent had done in the century before. At least Hood's work was available to the American reader, if not the British. In Canada, Peter Morgan painstakingly collected together Hood's letters and published them, with an introduction and notes, in 1971 – an invaluable contribution to Hood studies. But still Hood's would-be British readers were blocked in their efforts to acquire his verse until, in 1970, Julian Ennis published his selection, *Whimsicalities and Warnings*. In 1982, Pavel Büchler's illustrated selection, *Hoodwinked*, once more brought to life *Sally Simpkin's Lament*, *Faithless Sally Brown*, *Faithless Nelly Gray*, *The Sausage Maker's Ghost*, and *I Remember, I Remember*. But neither of these volumes has brought about the hoped-for revival of a body that seems, as yet, well and truly dead.

Who, then, killed Thomas Hood? It is manifest from what we have said that it was not his nineteenth-century publishers, nor a want of editors and critics. The numerous editions of his works published in that century testify to that. *What*, then, killed Thomas Hood? Certainly the change of intellectual climate after 1918 had something to do with the change in attitude towards much else that was Victorian. The fragmentation of art brought about by the search for new forms of expression, such as Cubism, Dadaism, and Surrealism, the effect on writers of the recently-exhibited paintings of the Post-Impressionists, the newly-translated works of Russian authors such as Dostoyevsky, and the revolutionary theories of Freud and Marx, all helped to contribute to a modernist age that was to produce James Joyce's *Ulysses*, T.S. Eliot's *The Waste Land*, the novels of D.H. Lawrence, and the poetry of W.H. Auden. In these more sophisticated times, puns were very low currency, common to the patter of comedians, and the literary-minded looked to more subtle, and even more frivolous, forms of humour to amuse themselves. The pun was a paradox, at once too serious and too

144

trivial. Hood's reputation for punning, so endemic in his particular kind of genius, has since closed in on his serious romantic poetry, as it has on his skills as an engraver and etcher, and, leech-like, will not let go. To parody 'Cock Robin', we might resolve the fatal question thus:

> Who killed Tom Hood?
>   I, said the pun,
>   With my double fun
> I killed Tom Hood.

As to "Who'll dig his grave?" the answer is that it has already been dug, perhaps by the editors, the critics, or even the readers, each in his own way. But Hood will not let us have the last word. In reply to the question "Who'll toll the bell?" he silences all criticism of puns with the most sublime of all puns, in those justifiably famous and remarkably prophetic lines from *Faithless Sally Brown*:

> His death, which happen'd in his berth,
>   At forty-odd befell,
> They went and told the sexton, and
>   The sexton toll'd the bell.

Writing to Thomas Noon Talfourd in January 1841 on the subject of copyright, Hood, in summing up the plight of the impoverished and exploited author, was painfully aware of the pattern of his own end:

> So much for the honours paid to a literary man, during his life – if it can be called life, that so often is hardly a living. He writes for bread – & gets it short weight. For money – & receives the wrong change. For the present – & he is pirated. For the future – and his Children are disinherited for his pains. At last he sickens, as well he may, & can write no more. He makes his will – but as regards any literary property, might as well die intestate… And so he dies – a beggar perhaps – with the world in his debt. Being poor of course – he is buried with less ceremony than Cock Robin.[98]

Admired by so many great contemporaries, Hood's poetry deserves a re-appraisal. He was a poet of an unusual order of brilliance and invention. In amongst the twelve volumes of the *Complete Works*, we can search beneath the veil of contemporary reference and perilous punning to find a body of work that is worthy of a more respected place in our literature. Hood's daughter, Frances Freeling Broderip, praised his 'pure, intelligible English. He speaks in his works to the great mass of the people in a tongue they can understand and thoroughly feel.' Perhaps the last word should be given to one of his greatest admirers, the Victorian writer, Walter Savage Landor:

> Jealous, I own it, I was once.
> That wickedness I hear renounce.
> I tried at wit, it would not do;
> At tenderness, that fail'd me too;
> Before me on each path there stood
> The witty and the tender Hood.

PART TWO

THOMAS HOOD'S

THE PROGRESS OF CANT

First presented as a research paper for a seminar at King's College London in 1973. First printed in *Papers in Research and Criticism,* Polytechnic of Central London, 1976.

Caricature and Social Protest

'My dear friend,' remarked Dr Johnson to Boswell in 1783, 'clear your mind of cant.' In these words, he expressed a point of view close to the hearts of those men of the late eighteenth century to whom the hypocrisy and the vanity of the age were utterly abhorrent. For men of radical persuasion, the new notion of freedom was more aptly expressed in the fateful pages of Rousseau's *Contrat Social*: man was born free, and everywhere he was in chains. Thomas Paine's *The Rights of Man*, an answer to Burke's attack on the French Revolution, was symptomatic of the slow and painful transformation (at least in England) from aristocracy to democracy. Byron, apprehensive about the first Canto of *Don Juan*, wrote to Hobhouse that the poem was 'as free as La Fontaine; and bitter in politics, too; the damned cant and Toryism of the day may make Murray [his publisher] pause... When I say free, I mean that freedom which Ariosto, Boiardo, and Voltaire – Pulci, Berni, all the best Italian and French – as well as Pope and Prior amongst the English – permitted themselves'.[99] As early as 1759, Sir Joshua Reynolds had complained bitterly of the "cant of criticism" prevalent among the diehards of the literary and artistic salons of the day.[100] As the 'Age of Cant' was set precariously, and then more resolutely, on its path, the bitter voices of the squib-hacks, the poetasters, the 'literary' caricaturists came to be heard in their hundreds, harassing, vilifying and mercilessly lampooning the leading figures of the day. So began one of the most remarkable revolutions in the history of criticism, a long and cruel battle of scathing wit which, by its increasing power and ferocity, was to alter not a little the course of England's political, social, and to some extent, literary and artistic life. Echoing the words of Reynolds, Sterne passionately proclaimed: 'Of all the cants which are canted in this canting world, though the cant of hypocrites may be the worst, the cant of criticism is the most tormenting.'[101]

There is no more entertaining way of unravelling the complex themes of the Age of Cant than by examining the work of its caricaturists. To the beginner, the task may seem daunting, for there are thousands of caricatures, many of which satirise obscure topical issues long since forgotten. A skill in the interpretation of the images and symbols can be acquired only by application and *reading*, for caricatures require to be *read*, not merely visually scanned for form and line, as we would do with other art forms. For example: an enormous baby, ailing and fractious, lies in his cradle, tended by a grotesque nurse and surrounded by costly toy soldiers in exotic uniforms.[102] The caricature is called 'The Great Babe', and by reading some of the clues and images we realise it is a caricature of George

IV (later known as 'The Dandy of Sixty'), tended by one of his mistresses, Lady Conyngham; the toy soldiers remind us that the King has a passion for military uniforms, of which he had collected many for the royal wardrobe. As a visit to the Royal Pavilion at Brighton would show, the Prince Regent, his ministers, his mistresses, and eventually his Queen, all provided the insatiable caricaturist with his bitter sustenance, for the caricaturist was a parasite who lived on the backs of the famous as well as the infamous.

Queen Caroline was to become one of the most pathetic public figures of her time, victimised by King and Parliament, wandering aimlessly from country to country with no hope of vindication. The second daughter of the Princess Augusta (sister to George III), Caroline grew up a gentle though unprepossessing child, given to eccentricity. Forced to marry the dissolute Prince of Wales in 1795, she was lamentably persecuted by his mistresses, only to be deserted by her husband in the following year. Denied access to her child in 1813, she was allowed to travel abroad where, in Italy in 1814, she took into her service Bartolomeo Bergami and his relatives. Bergami became her constant companion and thus the subject of much scandal and caricature. On hearing of the death of George III, Caroline set out for England only to find on arrival that her name had been struck from the State prayers. In spite of being offered a settlement by which she should stay abroad and renounce her title as Queen of England, she entered London in June 1820 amidst great popular rejoicing, a reflection of the general contempt for the dissolute King. In July, a bill was put before the House of Lords by which the King would divorce her but, with popular feeling running so much in her favour, it was abandoned in November for fear of a revolution. Her final humiliation came on 29 July 1821, when she was forcibly excluded from the Coronation. Soon afterwards, she, in the presence of her lady-in-waiting, burnt her diaries (how fascinating they would have been!) and died broken hearted.

Caricaturists were not slow to record the sensational incidents of the Queen's life. One such incident arose subsequent to her trial when, not content with her modest triumph, she unwisely announced her intention of driving in state to St Paul's Cathedral to give thanks for her deliverance from the iniquitous charges brought by her husband. Attended by numerous trumpeters, stewards in their carriages and gentlemen of the court on horseback, the corpulent Queen proceeded on her way, followed by representatives of the various trades of the City carrying their flags and banners. Her most acrimonious critics were reminded of a journey she had previously undertaken to Palestine where she had made her entry into Jerusalem on a donkey, an action thought by some to be blasphemous in the extreme. The triumphal drive through London thus gave rise to one of the rarest of caricatures: *Grand Entrance to Bamboozl'em*.[103] The Queen heads the procession, mounted on a braying jackass. A figure (probably intended to be her friend and adviser Alderman Wood) is dressed in a fool's cap and jester's motley; a lady follows him, playing a fiddle and wearing a Scotch bonnet (her lady-in-waiting Lady Ann Hamilton); behind her come the Queen's Italian companion Bergami (after the trial, nicknamed 'Non Mi Ricordo') and his fat sister, whom the Queen had created a countess. Bergami carries a banner inscribed *Innocence*, a punning reference to Brougham's remark that the Queen was 'pure, in a sense'. Among the crowd, we spy Venus and Bacchus, who are labelled *Protégés and bosom friends of Her M[ajest]....y*. Dr Folliott, in a discussion on modesty in Peacock's *Crotchet Castle*, avers that *he* would not dream of sending his footman to school with a naked Venus. Mr Crotchet, contemptuous of such cant, has adorned his house with "the Greek Venus in all her shapes", and proclaimed that he was ready to "fight her battle against all the societies that ever were instituted for the suppression of truth and beauty"[104] The Queen is welcomed by an enthusiastic group of butchers with marrow bones and cleavers, while among the crowd we notice the orator and radical Henry Hunt, William 'Tompaine' Cobbett, and other popular demagogues.

Such prints accurately display the conflict between the nascent Victorian England and the unregenerate England of Georgian times. Furthermore, the Age of Cant, at its peak in 1820, showed the social fabric to be saturated with Evangelicalism and Neo-Puritanism.[105] Cant, as Byron saw it in 1822, was "the crying sin" of the age. Mr Crotchet was right to complain: "Sir, ancient sculpture is the true school of modesty. But where the Greeks had modesty, we have cant; where they had poetry, we have cant; where they had patriotism, we have cant; where they had anything that exalts, delights, or adorns humanity, we have nothing but cant, cant, cant".[106] Thus, for over three quarters of a century the battle raged between the established social order on the one hand, and, on the other, the radical determination to overthrow the old system of values and replace it with the new liberalism of the post-enlightenment.

Nothing now could stem the tide of vicious and outrageous attacks on the sins and vices of the ruling class, the monarchy and its fatuous antics however being redeemed only in the nick of time by the more sober William IV, and the vivacious young Princess Victoria. An increasing impatience with what Johnson had defined as a "whining pretension to goodness", namely cant,[107] had led in the 1820s to a flagrant abuse of the freedoms so cherished by the great architects of the Enlightenment. All hell seemed to be let loose in the print shops, with their abundant series of engravings, etchings and comic cuts depicting every shade of opinion, every event however trivial, every scandalous intrigue, every private secret in the lives of the famous, mercilessly pilloried for a penny plain or tuppence coloured, scurrilous *grotesqueries* reflecting the scorn and ridicule of the radical press, in the brilliant caricatures of Rowlandson, Gillray, Cruikshank and a host of others.

By 1830, the reaction had set in; an air of apathy and tranquillity prevailed, and a temporary reconciliation between ministers and people was manifest. By 1849, Thackeray, writing on the art of George Cruikshank, was recalling with nostalgia the old print shops of his youth:

> Knight's in Sweeting's Alley (Cornhill), Fairburn's in a court off Ludgate Hill, Hone's in Fleet Street – bright enchanted palaces, which George Cruikshank used to people with grinning, fantastical imps and merry harmless sprites – where are they?... the atrocious Castlereagh, the sainted Caroline (in a tight pelisse, and feathers on her head), the Dandy of Sixty, who used to glance at us from Hone's friendly windows – where are they?... How we used to believe in them! To stray miles out of the way on holidays in order to ponder for an hour before the delightful window in Sweeting's Alley! In walks through Fleet Street, to vanish abruptly 'down Fairburn's passage, and there make one at his 'charming gratis' exhibition! There used to be a crowd round the window in those days of grinning good natured mechanics, who spelt the songs and spoke them out for the benefit of the company, and who received the points of humour with a general sympathizing roar. Where are these people now? [108]

In reality, Thackeray's crowds outside the print shop were no more "good natured" than the outrageous and frequently uncivilised, even tasteless, humour of the many prints displayed to the mocking public. The grinning faces of the crowds were cleverly reflected in the grotesques and arabesques of the caricatures themselves. Thackeray appears, in his flush of nostalgia, to have rejected the reality in favour of the sentiment to such an extent that the Age of Cant was on the wane. Caricature became concerned with catchwords and competing enthusiasms which it stigmatised as humbug of the sporting world. In respect of the last of these, we are reminded of the passion with which Mr Pickwick, in reprimanding the forlorn Mr Winkle, on account of his ridiculous attempts to skate on the pond at Dingley Dell, finds it necessary to explain to Mr Winkle that he is not only, in cant terms, a humbug, he is also in plainer terms an impostor.[109] Winkle, who never claimed to be even a moderately good skater from the very beginning, is goaded into skating willy-nilly. He is thus the unwilling perpetrator of a grand deception and is finally exposed for what he *is*, rather than for what he is not. Pickwick is depicted as the arch-enemy of humbug, though ironically he is frequently the victim of it. Thus, in caricature, the interaction of the reality and the illusion is self-perpetuating, giving rise to a complex fabric of minute relationships and associations which appear more often than not, in the form of visual and verbal puns, known technically as 'points of humour'.

In a fertile mind like that of a Gillray, a Cruikshank, or a Hood, this associative technique (or mania as some would have it) is especially suited to the 'processional' kind of caricature, which allows for the maximum display of verbal and visual ingenuity. To a limited extent, this may be seen in Vandergucht's caricature (published by Benbow in June 1825) entitled *The Reign of Humbug*,[110] a rather confused design with poorly drawn figures, but a design nevertheless in which there is a superficial interplay of ideas: outside the Houses of Parliament members stand round a *Bottomless Pit of Popery* from which snakes are emerging. Over the pit is a windlass by which Lord Grey (the Prime Minister), dressed as a monk, pulls up a bucket heaped with papers marked *Petition* and *Catholic Emancipation*. Behind is Lord Brougham with a broom over his shoulder. Other figures include a man clasping an umbrella and holding out a book inscribed *Life 2nd Vol*. This is Pierce Egan, the phenomenally successful author of *Life in London* (an account of the adventures of "Corinthian Tom", Jerry Hawthorne, and their friend, Bob Logic). Round his neck hangs a pair of boxing gloves, for Egan's most successful work was *Boxiana*, an account of pugilism and the prize-fighters of the period, Tom Cribb, Molyneux, and many others. There are also references to bubble companies, lotteries, Quakers, Jews, the new railways, and the newly-erected London Bridge, but references which today, to the untrained eye, seem obscure and whose significance, therefore, persistently eludes us.

Topicality forms a barrier to our understanding of a caricature. It would, for example, assist our comprehension of the 'processional' graphic satire if we knew that processions had some special significance for Londoners in the 1820s. After Queen Caroline's acquittal, for example, the streets of the city were thronged with processions to Westminster to present Loyal Addresses to Parliament on behalf of the Queen. They came from the towns and the shires, from the boroughs and the parishes to make their opinions known. Enormous processions with banners and symbols, watched by crowds, marching from the east end of London to Brandenburgh House in Hammersmith, were a feature of the times "that manifested at once the energy and folly of democracy in its wildest hour of excitement. This army of working men with banners and placards headed by deputations of their committees with wands of office – all terribly in earnest – all perfectly convinced of the Queen's immaculate purity – all resolved that oppression should not triumph – a peaceful multitude, but one that in any other country would have seemed the herald, if not the manifestation of Revolution".[111]

The most remarkable 'processional' caricature of the period is, without doubt, *The Progress of Cant* by a (then, and it appears now) little-known engraver and etcher, Thomas Hood, who was later to be more widely known for his whimsical humour, his irrepressible predilection for punning, his brilliant poems *The Dream of Eugene Aram, Miss Kilmansegg and her Precious Leg*, and the popular, *I Remember*. *The Progress of Cant* is, as I have said, remarkable. A large etching, bristling with allusions, it is a satirical comment on the principal topics of the day: organised philanthropy, sabbatarianism, puritanism, evangelicalism, prison welfare, liberty of the press, bubble companies, education, universities, Greek affairs, and the Reform Act, to name only a few. Hood wrote to his mother-in-law from Islington on 9 November 1825, apologising for not posting his letter to her the day before, "but the time went by whilst I was over my picture. - You, who are an Artist know [how] difficult it is to leave off whilst you have all your subject in your mind's eye. - The drawing (as they say of the lottery) will be over today, - and I am very well satisfied, - such is my vanity with its effect".[112] Hood was justified in his pride, as his critics have since affirmed.

> A wicked wag has produced a caricature... in which he marshalleth all the projected movements of the age, and maketh them take their fantastic progress before the eyes of the scorner. It is a spirited etching, almost as abundant in meaning as in figures... Priests, anti-priests, architects, politicians, reformers, flaming-loyalty men, high and low, rich and poor, one with another, all go on "progressing"...[113]

The *London Magazine* was full of praise:

> We have been exceedingly delighted with an etching... which will, or we are greatly mistaken, attract very considerable notice, from its singular and happy humour of design, and felicity of execution. We can fearlessly say, that we know of no production so nearly approaching to the admirable works of Hogarth, in their forcible delineations of nature, and their comic and pungent satire, as this etching of "The Progress of Cant"... Someone has said, and said truly, that "Hogarth's pictures we *read*". We may say the same of the picture before us. A mere look at it will be insufficient, for there is enough to delight and amuse the *reader* for hours... and considering that it has been planned, drawn and etched by the same person, we confess we do

not a little admire the patience, genius, and skill of the author.[114]

Before attempting a description of the etching, it is worth remembering that 1975 marked the 150th anniversary of the publication of Hood's first volume of poems, *Odes and Addresses to Great People*, which he wrote in collaboration with his brother-in-law, John Hamilton Reynolds. The occasion went unnoticed by critics and academics alike. In the course of that time, no critic has given much attention to *The Progress of Cant*, beyond a passing reference or two. Hood's art as an etcher, and designer of over nine hundred wood-cuts, has been neglected in favour of his poetry and comic verse. A number of respected critics have given credence to the theory that Hood diversified his talents too much. Others have entirely disregarded the infinite variety of his work as an artist. What is abundantly clear is that his genius from the very beginning of his career manifested itself in its diversity in serious copperplate engraving under the expert guidance of his uncle, Robert Sands; in parody and satire; in punning verses of unparalleled brilliance; in macabre ballads like *The Dream of Eugene Aram*; in hundreds of pictorial puns (the precursors of the *Punch* cartoons); and in eleven stout volumes of poetry and prose. Among his many distinctions, we may regard *The Progress of Cant* as one of his greatest achievements, and since its figures are closely linked to themes and images in the *Odes and Addresses* we can safely assume that the etching was intended as a frontispiece to the work. It is therefore also of the greatest *literary* interest, for the etching serves as a valuable key to the growth of the poet's mind.

THE PROGRESS OF CANT. Published by Thomas McLean, 26 Haymarket, 1825. Designed & Etched by one of the Authors of 'Odes and Addresses to Great People'.

'The Progress of Cant' – colourised version of Thomas Hood's engraving of 1825

By kind permission of Aberdeen University

Left-hand section of *The Progress of Cant*

Central section of *The Progress of Cant*

157

Right hand section of *The Progress of Cant*

158

A Masterpiece of Caricature

The Progress of Cant is an intricate design with a complex network of inscriptions, and it is sufficient for our purposes to attempt an explanation of the human figures only, for space does not allow adequate study of the background with its crumbling edifices (out of which rise the foundations of the new St. Pancras Church). Nor can we spare the time to investigate the many topical graffiti on the walls, and we must further resist the temptation to explain the titles of the pile of books at the feet of the first figure. It is sufficient to say that not the smallest detail is wasted; everything in the etching is intensely relevant. "The print, wherein our beadle is foremost, though not first", wrote Hone, "is one of the pleasantest 'droll' of the century, and seems to hit at all that is".[115] In the foreground, a procession with banners moves slowly from right to left, joined by another procession from the middle distance.

Clearly we are witnesses of a great pilgrimage – a pilgrimage rather than a procession, the pilgrimage of the large mass of the people who were, like the bedraggled elector seated on the post at the end of the procession, painfully, despairingly, progressing towards a new vision of life, just as Chaucer's pilgrims had set out for ***Cant**erbury* centuries before, but their journey is joyless and devoid of hope. They can never escape their condition. They are under-privileged and 'Under Government'.

The following notes describe the figures depicted from the end of the procession (at the right hand end) to the head (left hand end):

1. A bedraggled, drunken reveller, a rake of the political kind, with bandaged head and a bludgeon under his arm, rests on a post inscribed *Under Government MDCCCXXV*. In his hat is an election favour with the inscription *Purity of Election*. From his pathetic air of dejection, we understand that he is one of the corrupt oppressed, and symbolises the state of the nation prior to the electoral reform and the weeding out of the rotten boroughs such as Old Sarum. On the ground is a paper: *To the Worthy and Independent Electors of Old Sarum... Civil and Religious Liberty... Public Principles... Conscientious Vote... Reform.* Hone writes: "The villainous countenance of the intoxicated wretch is admirable". From his pocket hangs a purse full of money, possibly paid to him as an election bribe, or possibly denoting that he has just returned from the war, a survivor from Waterloo, perhaps, hence the pointedness of the chalking on the wall behind him: *Ask for War* (the edge of the etching obliterates the rest of the advertisement for *Warren's* blacking. There are several instances in which we are asked to supply the missing pun. The reveller is underprivileged

and "Under Government". In this sense, as Hone suggests, he is an admirable example of the radical propaganda, and as Dorothy George suggests in her monumental *Catalogue of Political and Personal Satires*, the Address to the Electors of Old Sarum "derides the doctrine of the perfection and inviolability of the Constitution".[116]

2. Beside the dissolute elector, who appears in no manner to be one of the elect in the religious or any other sense, stands a sanctimonious man in quasi-clerical dress, a representative of Hannah More's Religious Tract Society, founded in 1799. He carries a pamphlet entitled *Eternity*, so rolled as to look like a pistol, which he tenders to the besotted elector. His pocket is bulging with other homilies entitled *Pious Thoughts* and *True Elect*. It is fair to say that Hannah More's plans to save the poor by feeding them with religious principles was, as Cobbett tartly expressed it, meant to teach them "to starve without making a noise" (*Political Register*). Perhaps Pusey's 1833 *Tract* on fasting might have provided them with food for thought eventually, but certainly little else.

3. A French fruit-seller, a common sight in the streets of London after Waterloo, sells fruit from a tray slung over his shoulders. He wears a Phrygian cap (the badge of the Jacobins) and slippers, and beside him an evil looking companion with straggly hair, striped trousers, and a patch over one eye, carries a banner inscribed *Bethel Union*, a Baptist Missionary Society founded by George Woolcot.[117] The Roguish pair are none other than the villainous Robert Macaire and his accomplice Bertrand, both of whom were brilliantly caricatured by Daumier. In English caricature, Frenchmen were seen to be lean, and were shown to feed on frogs and *soupe maigre*. Italians were foppish and usually villainous, as can be admirably seen in Cruikshank's caricature of Bergami in Hone's political satire *Non Mi Ricordo*. In one print of the period, a squib concerning the Queen's Affair reads:

> Two hundred Ragg'd Italians
> With dancing bears and mice,
> Prepar'd for any dirty job
> And for all sorts of vice.[118]

The English were similarly dealt with in French caricatures of the period, though with less artifice and bite.

6   5 4

4. In front of the fruit-seller, a fat schoolboy with a banner inscribed *Missionary Penny Subscriptions* eyes the expensive fruit, which he cannot afford since he has paid his last penny to the Sunday School collection for Foreign Missions. Charles Lamb, with his amazing eye for detail, noticed that the boy's fingers were curled round in the bottom of his pocket, thus showing its genuine emptiness. Subscriptions to missions in far-off places were described aptly by Dickens as 'Telepathic philanthropy'. Not only do we have Mrs Jellyby's obsessive devotion to the natives of Borrioboola-Gha (to such a degree that her pathetic daughter is moved to cry: "I wish Africa was dead!,"[119] we also have Mrs Pardiggle's devotion to the Tockahoopo Indians, the whole race being supported, it seems, by weekly contributions from the pocket money of the eldest of her five small sons. The rest, we are told, were constrained to pay up weekly to the Great National Smithers Testimonial, the Superannuated Widows, and the Infant Bonds of Joy. They were, says Dickens, "ferocious with discontent".[120]

5. Behind the fat boy is a solid, square-faced man holding a banner inscribed *Savings Bank*, a reference to the growing popularity of the idea that the poor could be saved by savings. "The benefit clubs, among artisans, having accumulated stocks of money for their progressive purposes, a plan was adopted to identify these funds with the public debt of the country, and an extra rate of interest was held out as an inducement; hence were formed savings banks to receive small sums, returnable with interest on demand".[121] By 1840, 550 such banks had been established. Hood's figure here appears to be that of an artisan.

6. Next comes a lank-haired sectary bearing a banner inscribed *Whitfield and Wesley*. He wears a Puritan hat, frock coat, and with a wicked smile, points up to a banner marked *Fry for Ever*, a grim warning to sinners. From his pocket hangs a kerchief on which are the words *O Let us lay hold of Sal*, Sal being a popular name for a prostitute (as in Pall-Mall Sal in Hood's poem *A Nocturnal Sketch*), who is here denied Sal-vation.

163

11   10

9   8   7

13

7. The 'frying' pun (!) refers to Elizabeth Fry, the prison reformer and Quakeress, who is seen farther along the procession as a matronly tailor's dummy. Indeed, the fat trollop or bawd in front of the sectary is a travesty of Mrs Fry, with ragged dress and broken scissors. Her identity, however, is somewhat of an enigma. Briefly, her low-cut dress, her large, bare arms, her ample bosom, her sensual lips, the outrageous way in which she shows her ankle (enough to excite a lustful passion in many a Victorian male), all these suggest that she is intended to represent a prostitute. Her beauty spots, however, suggest that she may be of aristocratic or even royal blood. The

London Magazine thought she might be Lady Barrymore crusading against the spread of 'blue ruin' (gin), dressed as an inmate of Bridewell Prison.

8. Since she is stepping on the tail of the Devil, on the other hand we might reasonably suppose her to be a cruel caricature of the Queen herself, stepping on the tail of a Mephistophelean Wilberforce, who had attempted a compromise in the matter of the divorce action. His support of the abolition of slavery explains his banner inscribed *Freedom for the Blacks*. Caricaturists often depicted Caroline as a criminal, deprived of all her rights and privileges as Queen. One of the more outspoken caricatures showed her as a naked hag, with Pitt as Death, and the King as a menacing skeleton.[122] In Hood's fertile imagination, the figure of Lady Barrymore is more than likely to have fused with that of the Queen, and clearly here with that of Elizabeth Fry, seen as one of the female prisoners she strove to help in the degrading and insanitary conditions of Newgate, a place, she told the House of Commons, of "begging, swearing, gaming, fighting, singing, dancing, dressing-up in men's clothes",[123] entirely unfit for young persons. Hone thought the caricature of the Caroline-Barrymore-Fry figure worthy of Hogarth himself.[124]

9. In front of the Devil, we see one such young person, one of Mrs Fry's assistants, slim and demure in a Quaker bonnet, and carrying a banner *Newgatory Instruction*, an indication of her nugatory efforts to teach the female prisoners.

10. Above the young girl, we see a sweep riding on an ass, his brush across his shoulder, like a rifle. He wears a white top hat, indicating that he is a follower of the radical politician, Henry Hunt, who took part in the Spa Fields riot, was an advocate of universal suffrage, and opposed John Cam Hobhouse's election to Parliament in February 1819. Hunt had shared rooms with Cobbett in gaol in July 1810, and now he was to be lodged at the New Bailey Prison in Manchester and committed for trial (hence the graffito on the wall to the right *Try Hunt*). On his retirement from Parliament, he devoted his life to the business of blacking manufacturer.

11. Next to the sweep, we see a bareheaded cleric with a banner inscribed *Let Every Child Have Its Bib*. As we have seen already in the example of *Ask for War*, there are a number of instances in the etching in which Hood deftly obscures part of a word, and here is another. The "reader" is left to supply the pun himself. Bible Societies flourished at the turn of the century. The British and Foreign Bible Society was founded in 1803, the City of London Auxiliary Bible Society in 1806, and many others, so many in fact

that Pope Pius VII issued a Bull against them in June 1816, thus exciting much animosity among zealous evangelists.

12.Now we come to the grim, square-jawed man who joins the affray. He is one of the Irish rioters who took part in the violent elections of 1825. The *London Magazine* describes him as "a shirtless Hibernian, who is carrying the flag of *Irish Conciliation*".[125]

13. Watching the affray, is a bare-legged Scotsman in a very short (transparent) kilt. He carries a double banner: *Scotch Charity* and *Naked and Ye Clothed Me*, the motto of the Charity Schools. One such institution was the Caledonian Asylum for the children of 'indigent, respectable' parents, founded at Islington in 1813. A caricature entitled *State of the Money Market*[126] depicts England as John Bull in agonised alarm as Bank buildings are crashing round him, whilst Scotland is seen in the figures of two complacent bankers raking in sovereigns and notes. The text beneath contrasts the perfect stability of Scottish banks with the banking failures in England, where a banking crisis in late 1825 had been caused by over-speculation. Here, Hood appears to be showing us an Englishman in an ill-fitting kilt, representing the charity of the Scottish banks when the fiscal system of England was stripped naked. A further meaning may have been apparent to the 'reader' of 1825, for only three years before, the fat and by now corpulent King had paid a visit to Scotland and unwisely decided to appear dressed in a kilt at a royal levee, in company with Alderman Wood.[127] The event gave the caricaturists a field-day.

14. In front of the Scotsman, a representative of the *United Schools* falls to the ground – the Quaker flag-bearer of *Peace to the World*, who writhes in agony, victim of a "peace which the world cannot give".

15. In the midst of the affray, oblivious of the angry shouts of the artisans, stands a bloated tailor's dummy in the shape of Mrs Fry, wearing a heavy chatelaine of prison keys, scissors (this time not broken) and a pin cushion. Her apron bears the label *Made by the Females in Newgate*, but the effects, as we have seen, were "Newgatory".

16. In June 1814, the British and Foreign School Society held an anniversary meeting for which Mary Russell Mitford, author of *Our Village*, wrote a special poem entitled "The March of Mind". The Society, originally called the Lancastrian Society after its founder, Joseph Lancaster, sought to spread the Lancastrian system of education among the children of the poor, and was thus in competition with Dr Bell's 'Madras System' for educating the poor "in the Principles of the Church".[128] The pathetic

creature which Hood chooses to represent as the result of such propaganda is in striking contrast to the caricature drawn by Cruikshank to represent "The March of Intellect" in which big-headed, bespectacled boys with trumpets, drums, and banners, goose-step after their leader. In 1825, Lord Brougham founded the Society for the Diffusion of Useful Knowledge, and thus brought about the march of mind and intellect that was to characterise the new education for the masses. Peacock cleverly parodies the movement in *Crotchet Castle* in the 'Steam Intellect Society.'[129] In Hood's figure, the cretinous features, the crippled limbs, the rulers for crutches, the patched and ragged coat and breeches, are more than adequate testimony to prove the adage that 'a little learning is a dangerous thing'. The march of the mind has degenerated to the crawl of the cretin; the human being is degraded almost beyond recognition, little better than the dog which precedes it, and to which it bears an uncanny resemblance.

16   15   14   12

22   21   20   19   18   17

17. The procession is joined by another group of figures moving in from an adjacent street. Near the corner of the house on the right we see a jockey mounted on a blind and wretched-looking nag with a braided mane. He is whipping a small boy with his crop. The boy is trying to climb onto the horse, and carries a banner inscribed *No Climbing Boys*, a reference to the recent Chimney Sweep Act. Until 1840, it was still lawful for a master-sweep to take apprentices under the age of sixteen, and the usual practice was to take them as early as five or six years of age, since smaller boys were able to negotiate the dangerous twists and turns of the Victorian chimneys.

18. The sadistic jockey's banner proclaims *Martin for Ever*, for Richard Martin, Member of Parliament for Galway, was founder of the Society for the Prevention of Cruelty to Animals (1824). The ironic twist here is the jockey's inhumanity to man. Martin was a close friend of the King's, and was nicknamed 'Humanity' Martin by him. His fiery Irish temper no doubt explains the vicious expression on the jockey's face.

19. Beyond the jockey, a gesticulating youth waves his hat in the air, while two pugilists, stripped to the waist as was customary at prize-fights, engage in a battle of fisticuffs. The banner *No Pugilism* refers to the cant connected with the various opposing factions who wished to support or ban public contests. Pierce Evan's *Boxiana; or Sketches of Antient and Modern Pugilism*(1812-13) appears at a time when prize-fighting was at its zenith of popularity. Thousands flocked to see a contest with 'Gentleman' Jackson (from whom Byron took lessons), whilst as many would trek miles on foot to watch a fight between the black boxer Molyneux and the celebrated Tom Cribb, praised by Tom Moore.[130]

20. Next, a short-sighted, bespectacled Jew, wearing two hats, carries a pole topped by the traditional pawnbroker's sign, reversed ironically to make a Christian Cross. (A reference to the new movement for the conversion of the Jews). The two hats show he has a second-hand clothes shop, where it was customary to pile up the hats one upon the other on the counter. He is here protesting at the cant surrounding the position of Jews in 1825, for they were underprivileged, finding it difficult to get work except in their traditional trades of tailoring and pawn-broking. Further along the procession a poor Jew is seen picking pockets. The banner announces *The Equitable Loan* Company, which was floated to protect the poor from exploitation by pawnbrokers, mostly, as we have seen, Jewish. Vested interests were alarmed, but the scheme was given moral support by Elizabeth Fry and her husband, Joseph Fry. Hence, its promoters were caricatured as "Quakers, Jews, Heathens, Incendiaries, Usurers and Monopolists, a godly Fry". Nathan Rothschild, the financier and merchant,

was grossly caricatured as the balloon-maker, a convenient image for the spurious bubble company. The mention of 'Incendiaries' is a direct criticism of the Company's Chairman, Sir William Congreve, MP, inventor of the Congreve Rocket. Caricatures do not tell us a great deal about the wealthier Jews, who were mainly Sephardim, but the poorer Jew was an obvious target. "In London the old-clothes-man was part of the daily scene. With a pile of hats on his head and a sack over his shoulder, he could be seen and heard in every street and alley and his appearance in perpetuated in the many books of London Street Cries, while in the caricatures he was the Jewish stereotype".[131]

21. Beside the Jew, a ragged man with a bandaged head carries a banner *Gall and Spurs-him*, clearly emphasising the jockey's brutal dig with his spur against the climbing-boy's knee, and against the lean flanks of the listless nag. However, the reference is to the current craze for Phrenology, the study of the human skull as being indicative of mental powers and moral qualities. The system was propagated by the German physician, Dr Gall, in 1803. During the years 1813-17, Dr Spurzheim (Spurs-him) visited England and popularised what he called the *Physiognomical system of D Gall and Spurzheim*. Samuel Carter Hall remembered meeting Coleridge in Paternoster Row on his way to see Spurzheim who pronounced Coleridge a mathematician, and in no way a poet!

22. A diminutive figure with his head eclipsed by his hat bears a banner *The Great Unknown*, and holds a switch (for changing the points on railway tracks) 'points of humour' as we have said! In his pocket is a constable's staff surmounted by a crown, a valuable clue to the figure's identity – he is Sir Walter Scott, whose 'Waverley' novels were published anonymously. In 1818, Ann Scott dubbed him 'The Great Unknown', whose disagreement with his publisher, Archibald Constable, ended with a threat to 'switch' to another.

23. In 1817, Sir William Cubitt introduced the ancient Chinese treadwheel into England, thus, with canny ingenuity, converting an invention for irrigating land into a cruel punishment for felons. A treadmill was duly introduced into Brixton Gaol in the same year.[132] Here we see an old one-legged, one-armed sailor treading the streets of London begging for alms, a familiar sight in the days of high-rigged vessels, when amputation without anaesthetics were commonplace occurrences at sea. 'Jemmy' Catnach, the ballad-printer of St Giles, published an illustrated penny broadside, *The Treadmill*, on 15 November, 1822.[133]

170

25   24

23

24. We now have a grinning funeral mute who holds up his crepe-crested staff, to which is attached a streamer inscribed *No Life in London*. Hone describes him as a "Jovial undertaker in his best grave-clothes", and wryly comments that "this character looks as if he would bury his wife comfortably in a country churchyard, get into the return-hearse with his companions, and crack nuts and drink wine all the way to town".[134] Pierce Egan's phenomenally successful *Life in London* followed the adventures of Corinthian Tom, Jerry Hawthorne and Bob Logic from high life to low life, from the grand drawing-rooms of the aristocracy to the grim taverns of the poor at Seven Dials. Raffish young men began to imitate Tom and Jerry, to copy their dress, their speech and their habits. Between 1821 and 1840, at least ten dramatic productions were staged in London, and many more went unrecorded.[135] The work's success was sociological rather than literary, its effect being largely on language, manners and conduct. The adventures of Tom and Jerry were denounced from the pulpit on a charge of immorality. Seven years later, in *Finish to the Adventures of Tom, Jerry, and Logic in their Pursuits through Life in and out of London*, Egan sought to profit by the furore of 1821 by adding a clumsy moral to the sequel.

25. A minister in gown and bands is clearly Edward Irving, with his notorious squint. His melodious voice, imposing presence and commanding stature, made him a popular preacher at the Hatton Garden Chapel, the church of the established Church of Scotland in London, connected with the Caledonian asylum for the children of indigent but respectable parents. The flag-bearer of the Caledonian chapel stands behind, tossing up a halfpenny with the standard-bearer of *No More State Lotteries*. Irving's followers, the Irvingites, founded the Holy Apostolic Church, resulting in Irving's suspension by the Synod of the Church of Scotland on a charge of heresy. Here Hood sees him as *The Caledonian Chap* – preaching one of his popular sermons against the wickedness of the London stage, a sermon which annoyed the King enough for a royal command performance of 'The Hypocrite' to be performed. Repeated attacks were made on Hood throughout his life for his freethinking attitudes. Evangelical Christians, like Rae Wilson, to whom Hood wrote a bitter ode in 1837, strongly objected to Hood's portrayal of Irving as a figure of caricature.[136] A close scrutiny of the figures reveals a further subtlety. Irving's right eye looks askance at the noisy Lottery man, standing on tiptoe with excitement, as he watches the coin rise and fall, thus linking all three figures. Hood's reference is to the hypocrisy of sermonising against lotteries on the one hand, and the fact of the founding, by a state lottery in 1813, of the Caledonian Asylum, on the other. It might also be observed that Irving is showing a shapely leg adorned with garter, clocked stocking, and a fancy buckled shoe, a reference to the handsome Irving as Don Juan, for he was

deeply in love with Jane Welsh, but was engaged to Isabella Martin, whom he reluctantly married eleven years later in October 1823. Irving introduced Jane to his friend, Thomas Carlyle, whom she eventually married.

28   27   26

29, 30

26. A bespectacled man (John Cam Hobhouse) carries a banner *The Cause of Greece* exactly in line with that of the overfed incumbent of a nonconformist parish. His banner is inscribed ironically *No Fat Livings* (thus linking 'fat' and 'grease'). Hobhouse, a close friend of Byron's, was

one of the members of the Greek Committee set up to arrange a loan of £2,000,000 to provide a naval force for Greece, in her struggle for independence from the Turkish yoke.

27.   The popularity of processions through the streets of London, especially by representatives of the trades and professions, has already been alluded to. Now we have in this jumble of canting figures a printer in his paper cap, his face covered by a mask, implying the anonymity of the Press. He carries aloft a banner inscribed *The Liberty of the Press*. By the reign of George IV, the press had so much freedom that radical attacks on the monarchy reached unparalleled ferocity, but this period of licence was brought to an end by the 'Six Acts', otherwise known as the 'Gagging Acts' (1819-20).

28.   A barrister wearing his wig of office and brandishing a bludgeon upholds *Catholic Claims*. This is Daniel O'Connell with his shillelagh, a symbol of his powerful personality and rhetoric. Though he viewed the prospect of a union between Protestant and Catholic in Ireland as desirable, the old feud was revived with the defeat of the Catholic claims. O'Connell disillusioned, took up the claims of the poor unprotected Irish peasants, who were smarting under the power of the Protestant Ascendancy, and the Catholic Association was founded, thus taking "the first step out of servitude into nationality".[137]   The matter became a burning issue in 1825, the year of the *Progress of Cant*, when, on 10 February, the House of Commons passed the Catholic Relief Bill, only to be defeated in the House of Lords.

29.   It is clear from all we have said that the 'Age of Democracy' was a natural progression from the 'Age of Cant'. One battle-cry after another was added to the ever-lengthening list of radical propaganda. Catholic emancipation was yet another threat to the stability of the fast-fading principles of the old mid-18th-century world. The situation was brought to a head when the Duke of York rose to his feet in the House of Lords and defiantly cried: "No Popery!" Here was the glorious champion of Protestantism defending the Faith, and caricaturists were not slow in their response to the call. A veritable rash of prints appeared almost overnight, pillorying both sides of the argument, just as they had done during the Gordon Riots and those days of political unrest following the formation of the Protestant Association in 1779.

30.   The history of Catholic Emancipation is a long and complex one and can only be touched on briefly here. Hood depicts the oppressed

Catholic as a poor Charity Boy wearing a hat that is far too big for his diminutive head, and a pair of borrowed shoes.

34   33   32   31

31. Next to the boy, stands a rapacious-looking bishop with a banner *The Church is in Danger*, the 'D' being obscured by a banner marked *Converted Jews* and pointing to the anger felt on all sides in these complicated issues, instinct as they were with so much cant. The bishop in his lawn sleeves and canonicals is firmly standing his ground against Jews and Catholics alike.

32. The most prominent figure in the procession is the beadle, whom Hone thought one of the best things in the etching. With his "pudding sleeves, and collar, red as a beefsteak", he is "a walking refreshment".[138] He carries a nosegay as a defence against the evil-smelling poor, wears a passion-flower over his heart, and his staff of office is reversed to denote his being off-duty. He is "the very gem and jewel" in an etching of such "infinite fancy" illustrating the designer's views of the age of cant. At his heels, a savage dog barks and snarls at the *Vagrancy Act*, his collar marked *Office*, a reference to Hamlet's "Insolence of office".[139]

33. In front of the beadle, a dandy, wearing large spectacles and an elaborate hairstyle, is Hood's 'Doctor Darling' William Kitchiner, an authority on music, gastronomy, optics, and the art of prolonging life.[140] His banner *Let the Shop Close with the Jessamine* refers to the agitation by shop assistants in London to bring in early-closing, and extols the soothing qualities of jasmine tea. His embroidered coat, high collar, and his foot daintily pointed, as if he were dancing a stately minuet, show him to be a man of fashion.

34. He stares myopically through his patent spectacles at a man and woman embracing – not quite, we may suppose, the kind of 'mutual instruction' they would have received as the beneficiaries of the new movement towards adult education. In the *School for Adults*, such abundant charity is welcomed with open arms by the willing man, who accepts without question the woman's cant interpretation of *Goodwill to Men*. We also observe that the newly-educated *Adult* is so taken with his 'instruction' that he has forgotten the practical necessity of looking after his possessions. Here, as Baudelaire once described one of Hood's Cupids, a "great, chubby, dimpled Dolly" represents the popular idea of Love.[141] The figures may also be representatives of the Outinian Society (formerly the Matrimonial Society), whose aims were the improvement of married life.

37   36   35

35. A fat cretinous butcher with steel and cleaver holds a banner advertising *London University*. Beside him, an even fatter pig-faced boy is to be slaughtered on the altar of knowledge, dragging behind him his toy lamb on wheels. The London University was formed as a joint-stock company in 1825 and chartered in 1886. Lord Brougham, originator of the Society for the Diffusion of Useful Knowledge, was one of its founders. The University was satirised as 'Cockney College', where 'offal degrees' could be obtained by the sons of tradesmen at moderate fees. (There are several references in caricature and popular literature to knowledge thus gained as 'ham' and 'beef' at moderate prices). The project was seen as a dangerous challenge to the existing hierarchical system of education which placed Oxford and Cambridge at the top and Charity Schools at the bottom.

36. Next to the butcher is a carpenter in a paper cap (as in Tenniel's Illustration to Carroll's *The Walrus and the Carpenter*). His banner advertising *Nick's Institution* is a warning to all that Old Nick (the Devil) has entered the Hall of Education, though the reference is to the establishment of the London Mechanic's Institute (later Birkbeck College) in 1823.

37. Here, at this point in the procession, we may pause briefly to observe the waggoner, whose pennon obscures part of the mechanic's banner with the proclamation *Knowledge is Power*. Many people in high places feared that the widespread education of the poor would inevitably lead to the downfall of the nation and the sacrificing of the old freedoms and rights of the privileged classes. Some, however, genuinely feared that the whole of society would suffer, rich and poor alike, if the uneducated mass of the poor were educated too much, too fast. (We are reminded of the pathetic figure representing the March of Mind.) A fear of the poor was at the centre of much of the legislation passed by Parliament in Victorian times. "The feeling is that outside the sitting-room is an undefined world of wickedness, hunger, catastrophe and crime. Pick-pockets are nabbed, poachers are imprisoned, desperate labourers threatened arson, and children go to the mills and up the chimneys; the press gang and transportation are living memories, and sailors drown – oh, how many sailors drown! - in calamitous storms. These terrible things happen – to the poor. There we have Hood's background. There is his material."[142]

178

40   39   38

38. A second pick-pocketing Jew, a sandwich man, carries on his back a placard *Subscription for Putting down Bartlemy Fair*, a reference to the campaign to abolish the old Bartholomew Fair, since it attracted most of the pickpockets of London and was the scene of much corruption and immorality, in the eyes of the new evangelically-minded puritans. A puppet-Punch hands from the sandwich man's pocket: "Mr Punch, that godless old rebel, breaks every law and laughs at it with odious triumph, outwits his lawyer, bullies the beadle, knocks his wife about the head, and hangs the hangman – don't you see in the comedy, in the song, in the dance, in the ragged little Punch's puppet show – the Pagan protest?"[143]

39. The sandwich man faces a barber who stands outside his shop pointing to a tattered cloth hanging from the striped pole of his profession inscribed *Nobody Is To Be S-aved During D – ine Service By Command of the Magistracy*. A tear in the cloth has removed the 'h' of 'Shaved' and the 'iv' of 'Divine', making obvious puns available to those 'readers' who wish to see them. A fat woman, seated in a basket, with a squalling infant on her lap, sells fruit to two repulsive-looking brats. The clue to these figures lies in the newspaper on the ground. With the aid of a magnifying glass we can read: *New Times!!! Profanation of the Sabbath H Rickets and Sarah Grumpage the former for Shaving and the latter for selling fruit on the Lord's Day were convicted on the oath of the notorious Johnson and fines 10s. Each.* The Barber raises his palm outwards to the Jew, who hypocritically professes *The Preservation of Public Morals* whilst audaciously picking a pocket. Presumably, he is warning the Jew that even for him Sunday must be a day of rest.

40. At last we come to the head of the procession. A sturdy beggar, scantily dressed in rags, supports himself on a crutch, his right leg is bent back at the knee (a rarely authentic indication of incapacity). On his head, a bandage tells the public that he is *Crippled By A Injury from a Bear Bodkin*. The bodkin, or dagger, was a common symbol in caricature and stood for persecution; thus, like Hamlet, "he himself might his quietus make/With a bare bodkin".[144] A third layer to the pun is shown in the Mendicity Ticket which the beggar holds, for in 1818 the Mendicity Society for the suppression of begging was founded by, need we guess further, Sir William Henry Bodkin. It is of interest here to note that the beggar is the only one who stands facing the procession – perhaps to symbolise the utter futility of a society so instinct with cant and hypocrisy that it can surround the poor in a cloak of ragged philanthropy, and fail so miserably in its dubious humanitarian principles and aims.

THE BUILDINGS

The central image of Thomas Hood's etching shows new St. Pancras Church[*], erected in classical style indicated by the frieze of ox heads (bucicrania) , traditionally adorned with garlands and ribbons. They form part of the decoration on the north face of the Parthenon. Hood points to the controversy surrounding the adoption of such decoration by architect, William Inwood, for St. Pancras New Church, seen by some as inappropriate for the changing times. Inwood had further introduced a copy of the Erechtheum, with its four supporting caryatids, again a dominant feature of the Parthenon, and a major challenge to the anti-classicists.

Hood draws a parallel with the new Theatre Royal, Drury Lane, rebuilt in 1812, by adding his own version with, instead of caryatids, three elegantly attired society women, possibly actresses, but more likely to be the three principal mistresses of the Prince Regent (Mary Robinson, Mrs Fitzherbert (whom he later secretly married), and Lady Jersey).

We can safely assume that the Church had not been completed at the time when Hood was engraving his caricature, since he only lightly sketches in a proposed spire. A controversy arose after Inwood had visited Greece and saw the Temple of the Four Winds, which inspired him to adapt as his design to replace the idea of a spire.

---

[*] St Pancras New Church was built to serve newly built-up (developed) area close to Euston Road and well-to-do Bloomsbury. Project agreed 1816. Competition involving 30 or so tenders. Designs by local architect, William Inwood agreed on. Designed to seat 2500 people. Builder- Isaac Seabrook. First stone laid by Duke of York on 1 July 1816. Carved with Greek inscription: 'May the light of the blessed Gospel thus ever illuminate the dark temples of the Heathen.' [cf. Hood's theme in *Cant*. Consecrated 7 May 1822, three years before Cant!] Controversy - Total cost (land and furnishing) the colossal sum of £76,679. The most expensive church to be built in London since St Paul's Cathedral. Suppression of begging was founded by, need we guess further, Sir William Henry Bodkin. It is faced with Portland Stone (except stone tower and stone portico). External decoration in terracotta. Inwood's inspiration was the Erectheum (or Erechtheion) – two tribunes, each with entablatures supported by four caryatids. It is one of the most important 19th century churches in London.

THE PILE OF DISCARDED BOOKS (right-hand side, bottom)

At the back of the procession of canting protestors, Thomas Hood reminds us of some of the (in his view) canting controversial literature current in or about 1825. Perhaps he is placing the volumes there as suggestions for our future reading. It is more likely, however, that the books have been read and discarded. No-one can believe anything they read anymore.

Angelical Mag. 'Angel' may connect us to the name of the inn, '*The Angel and Punch-Bowl*', in the background of the etching, suggesting that for every word spoken we may take its opposite to be the truth. Where there is peace there is violence. Such is the duplicitous nature of cant. Religious cant, in Thomas Hood's view, was one of the worst forms of hypocrisy, as can be seen in his diatribe on Rae Wilson. Hence, here, a snipe at the *Evangelical Magazine*, which, according to Altick, sold from 18,000 to 20,000 copies in 1807 alone.[145]

Opie on Lying. Mrs. Amelia Opie (1769 - 1853), novelist and poet, was grand-daughter of the dissenting minister, J. Anderson and married the painter, John Opie. Her novel *Father and Daughter* (1801) roused great emotion among her readers, reducing Sir Walter Scott to tears. She met Charles James Fox in Paris and became friendly with Sheridan and Byron. Her life changed on meeting Joseph John Gurney, the 'Quaker pope', and she was formally received into the Society of Friends on 11 April 1825, after which she gave up novel-writing. In the same year, Longman published her *Illustrations of Lying in All its Branches*, a 'tract' which was circulated widely in America. In *Ode to W. Kitchiner, M. D.* Hood writes:

> Look at the Civic Palate — nay the Bed
> Which set dear Mrs. Opie on supplying
> 'Illustrations of Lying!'[146]

Horace and James Smith, in their phenomenally successful *Rejected Addresses*, composed a clever parody of an honest Address by the radical William Cobbett as 'The Hampshire Farmer' who admonishes the 'Most Thinking People' for expecting to be addressed politely as 'Ladies and Gentlemen' when they are, in fact, 'honest men and women'. In their parody of Samuel Johnson, 'Johnson's Ghost', they have Johnson criticising the Drury Lane Committee for sacrificing truth in praising the newly-finished theatre, when in fact 'he who should pronounce that our edifice has received its final embellishment would be disseminating falsehood without incurring favour.' The wealth of cant surrounding the building of the theatre appears again the parody of Samuel Taylor Coleridge, when they have the Rev. Rowland Hill preaching a sermon congratulating his congregation on the catastrophe and calling him 'a lying prophet.'[4] Clearly, here, Mrs. Opie's accusations are justified.

Kant. Thomas Hood almost certainly came to Kant through the writings of Samuel Taylor Coleridge, who he came to know as sub-editor of the *London Magazine*. But Kant's works were already widely circulated since the publication of his influential *Critique of Pure Reason* in 1781. Roughly, Kant's philosophy was based on the idea that knowledge derived from two sources: the senses (our sensuous perceptions) and the understanding. Concepts like space and time exist only through our consciousness, and are unified (or synthesised) only through our capacity for understanding. Secondly, we cannot arrive at the truth purely by the exercise of reason alone, because reason can lead us towards insoluble contradictions, such as the impossibility of conceiving limited or unlimited space. If abstractions of metaphysics fail us, at least the practicalities of reason can help us to distinguish the rights and wrongs in the maze of moral issues. Our 'moral consciousness' obliges us to take sides in the form of 'categorical imperatives' such as 'Do not lie.' It compels us to do all we can to promote the highest good in human beings. If we as individuals are subject to moral laws, then so is the world itself, responsible as it may be to a 'Master of the Universe'. At all events, 'Knowledge is Power', as the figure towards the head of the procession proclaims.

As Hone remarks: 'At the top [of the pile of books] is a large volume lettered "Kant", which, in such a situation, ...disciples of the German philosopher will only quarrel or smile at, in common with all who conceive their opinions or intentions misrepresented.'[147] In a nutshell, Kant's 'transcendentalism', which had spiritual connotations and therefore led to the consideration of questions of faith in nineteenth-century thinking, challenged the old eighteenth-century rationalist doctrines. We sense Hood's irritation with canting religious figures of the day in his poem. *An Open Question.* [148]

Spirit of Kant! have we not had enough
To make Religion sad, and sour, and snubbish,
But saints Zoological must cant their stuff,
As vessels cant their ballast — rattling rubbish! [7]

An edition of Kant's *Metaphysical Works*, translated by John Richardson came out in 1836, being a reprinting in one volume of separate works which had appeared in 1819. Immanuel Kant came from Königsberg, an enclave of Danzig (Gdansk), a town which traditionally carried on an exchange of craftsmen between continental Europe and Scotland. It is frequently stated the Kant's grandfather was of Scottish extraction, and the family name was originally Cant; but this story, though undoubtedly believed by Kant himself, is not generally credited by German philosophers.'[9]

Family Shakespeare. I do not remember my English master at Brentwood School being very backward in coming forward on the subject of 'Shakespeare's Bawdy'. However, to be taken in context, a great deal of delicate explanation had to be invented to gloss over some of its more salacious features. Nowadays, in times of sexual permissiveness, such caution would be considered gratuitous. Not so for Thomas Bowdler, whose *Family Shakespeare* was a defiant protest against the immorality of the stage, and in particular the productions of Shakespeare's plays. Thomas Bowdler (1754 - 1825) died in the year of *The Progress of Cant*, and would thus have been, like many of the events of that year recorded in this remarkable etching, much in Hood's mind as he took up his etching tool. Bowdler graduated as a Doctor of Medicine at Edinburgh University in 1776, a time that saw the rise of the great non-conformist movements. After travelling widely in Europe, he was elected a Fellow of the Royal Society in 178, and a Fellow of the Society of Antiquaries in 1784. Among his activities, he campaigned against the dangers of English invalids going for cures in French watering places, but in 1818 he took up the cudgel on behalf of the purity and innocence of children by his 'bowdlerised' version of Shakespeare's plays. *The Family Shakespeare in ten volumes: in which nothing is added to the original texts, but those words and expressions are omitted which cannot with propriety be read aloud in a family.* In the Preface, he has much to criticise in Shakespeare's language: 'Many words and expressions occur which are of so indecent a nature as to render it highly desirable that they should be erased.' He also complains of Shakespeare's frivolous allusions to the Holy Scriptures. Bowdler's prudery destroys much of the wit and earthy raillery of Shakespeare's original texts, and it was attacked in the *British Critic* for April 1822, to which Bowdler made reply: 'If any word or expression is of such a nature that the first impression it excites is an impression of obscenity, that word ought not to be spoken nor written or printed; and, if printed, it ought to be erased.'

Nevertheless, in spite of the cant surrounding the work, four editions appeared before 1824. Bowdler spent the last years of his life purifying Gibbon's *History of the Decline and Fall of the Roman Empire*, published just before his death in 1825.

Thomas Hood attacked the pious attitudes dissenters in his poem *Jarvis and Mrs. Pope,* in which Jarvis, the coachman, much given to swearing, receives a mere shilling for driving pious Mrs. Pope to chapel to hear a dissenting sermon:

> Not pious in its proper sense
> But chatt'ring like a bird
> Of sin and grace — in such a case
> Mag-piety's the word.
>
> He said a shilling was his fare,
> And wouldn't take no less —
> I said one shilling was enough —
> And he said C– U – S! [149]

Hood's daughter, Frances Freeling Broderip, wrote in her *Memorials of Thomas Hood,* that he warred against the professedly religious when they assumed the garb of piety, instead of charity, 'because anything false or hypocritical jarred on his sense of right.'

Hohenlohe. The clue to this enigma lies in a rare woodcut by George Cruikshank included as a frontispiece to *A Characteristic Portrait of Prince Hohenlohe working miracles.*[150] Printed for Knight and Lacey, Paternoster Row, and Wesley and Tyrrell, Dublin MDCCXXV, the year of *The Progress of Cant.* 'The altar of a Gothic cathedral is seen, the design framed in an ogival arch, supported by pillars. A large cobra has ascended the steps, puffing out smoke. In the foreground a fat monk blindfolds a woman. A cripple with gouty legs dances, balancing a crutch on his nose. Acolytes swing censers, fat monks and worshippers in tall conical hats face the altar. From the arches of the roof hang crutches and a wooden leg. The legend announces: *Prince Hohenlohe - Waldenburg (1794 - 1850) a Jesuit priest who claimed to effect miraculous cures by prayer, and who was in England about 1824.* He was ridiculed in *John Bull* in the 26 December issue. The porter in the woodcut has been identified as John Knox. A reported miracle cure seems to have taken place, according to Hone, in Somers Town (St. Pancras) in 1824.

Jones's Hymns.   John Jones was known as 'the people's preacher' and was one of nine children born to a small farmer in Carnaervonshire. He began preaching in the 1820s. Thought of as one of the greatest Welsh preachers, he attracted large congregations   His compositions were published in *Collection of Congregational Tunes, Psalms and Hymns*.[151] Jones was a supporter of the preacher, Rev. Alexander Fletcher during his trial. Jones is seen in Marks's engraving *Leaving Old Quarters – or – A March to Grub Street* (c. 1824). He is seen in procession, walking behind the Precentor and between tow goats, both bleating the word 'Wales'. He holds up a placard on a pole, 'Grub St. Ahoy'.

What is Prayers. Beneath the volume of Jones's compositions is a hymn-sheet with possibly an oblique and childishly illiterate reference to Isaac Watts's children's hymns and prayers.   Isaac Watts (1674 - 1748) was son of a non-conformist minister, author of 'Oh God, our help in ages past', and *Divine Songs attempted in easy language for the use of children,* which includes his warning against idleness:

> How doth the little busy bee
> Improve each shining hour,
> And gather honey every day
> From every opening flower![12]

But more appropriate here is his admonishment to children should they attempt to tell fibs:

> But liars we can never trust,
> Though they should speak the thing that's true;
> And he that does one fault at first,
> And lies to hide it, makes it two.[152]

Protruding from between 'Jones's Hymns' and 'What is Prayers', is a scroll inscribed **The Injured Foote.** The faint beginning of a clue to this figure may help us if we look at some lines in Hood's *Ode to Joseph Grimaldi, Senior.*[153]

> Ah, where thy ears, so often cuff'd! —
> Thy funny flapping, filching hands! —
> Thy partridge body, always stuff'd
> With waifs and strays, and contrabands! —

186

Thy foot — like Berkeley's *Foote* —
'Twas often made to wipe an eye!

We discover a further reference in Hood's *Ode to Maria Darlington,* on her return to the stage:

Unmolested by pea-colour'd Hayne!
And free from that thou-and-thee Berkeley![154]

The mystery is explained by the fact that the stage-part of Maria Darlington was played by Maria Foote, whom 'Pea-green' Haynes had to pay £3000 damages for breach of promise. The Quaker Colonel Berkeley, who was passionate about the stage and notorious for his gallantries to women, rushed to her defence, as Hood describes:

The man that could tread on a worm
Were a brute — and unhuman to boot;
But he merits a much harsher term
That can wantonly tread on a Foote!
Soft mercy and gentleness blend
To make up a Quaker — but he
That spurn'd thee could scarce be a *Friend*
Though he dealt in that Thou-ing of 'thee'.

Details of the deceit surrounding this *cause célèbre* are given by Everitt[155] It seems that Maria Foote was on tour in Cheltenham, a town much frequented by the dastardly Colonel Berkeley. He promised to marry Maria Foote (she had been his mistress for five years) on the understanding that he could not proceed further with the liaison while he was petitioning the Crown to restore a dormant peerage. Marriage to an actress might prejudice his cause. A rather 'silly fellow about town', Joseph Hayne, familiarly known for the colour of his pea-green coat, fell in love with the actress only to break off his engagement on learning of her affair with Berkeley. He later renewed it, broke it off yet again, but his passion for her was unquenchable. Eventually, a license was obtained. Maria sold her theatrical wardrobe. All was set for the wedding, but Hayne failed to appear. Maria issued a writ, recovered her £3000 damages and, after seven years, became the Countess of Harrington in 1831. She died in 1867. Hayne, because of his enormous income, was also known as 'Silver Ball', which accounts, after the trial on 21 December 1824, of 'Foote versus Hayne', for his sobriquet, 'Foote-Ball'. This accounts for a caricature *Miss Putting her Foot in it!! — or the Silver Ball.*[156] It is two designs side by side. In the first, a hideous man (Hayne) with long ass's ears slides his arm round Maria's waist. We notice she is pregnant. From his pocket projects a 'Foot Rule'. She holds a paper: 'Promise of Marriage'. A long document hangs from the table: 'Marriage Settlement'. Foote sits at the table, waiting to sign. Hayne says: 'my Angelic creature purer and more precious than the unsunned snow.' She says,' I accept that and the *pin money* is proof of your affection. Now sign the deeds and you shall have my affection.' In the second caricature, Maria, sitting in a rocking chair, is suckling an infant. Berkeley and Hayne stand on the other side of the room. Berkeley thumbs his nose at Hayne, raises two fingers and, with a grin and a pointed innuendo, mischievously remarks: 'I have been there before you, my boy. Take her if you like.'

Political Tracts   Hannah More began writing her *Cheap Repository Tracts* in 1792, with the publication of her enormously successful 'Village Politics', one of a long series of moral tales designed to drive out 'anti-Christian literature from the face of the earth.' 'Decked out with rakish titles and woodcuts [they were] sent out, like sheep in wolves' clothing, to be sold by hawkers in competition with their "old trash".'[157] The 'Tracts' were phenomenally successful, 300,000 being sold in the first six weeks. By March 1796, the total number reached the staggering figure of two million.   Two printing houses, Samuel Hazard's at Bath and John Marshall's in London were kept working to capacity. This was the age of the tract. Copies found their way into the poorest cottages and the richest mansions in the country. Radical anti-French tracts flourished during the Napoleonic wars as well as the Revolution. Edmund Burke's *Reflections on the French Revolution* appeared on 1st November 1790 and sold 30,000 copies. At least 38 pamphlets followed, embracing both conservative and radical viewpoints, the most influential being Tom Paine's *The Rights of Man*, which sold 50,000 copies within a few weeks. It was alleged that some 2000,000 copies were in circulation by1783 and by his death it was said that 1,500,000 copies had been sold.[158] The increasing popularity of the 'Jacobin' societies (mainly composed of middle class and skilled workmen who sympathised with the ideals of the French Revolution) helped to bring about an upsurge of protesting pamphlets of the political kind, so much so that, on 21 May 1792, a Royal Proclamation had to be passed against 'divers wicked and seditious writings'. Radical booksellers and pamphleteers were tried and imprisoned for disseminating subversive literature. The often scurrilous pamphlets of William Hone cruelly satirised the celebrities and events of the day. His partnership with the caricaturist, George Cruikshank, brought about a successful (and popular) series of political pamphlets such as *The Political House that Jack Built* (1819). Another political pamphleteer of interest was Richard Carlile (1790 - 1843), a freethinker, who issued Tom Paine's works in 1818.   Carlile was imprisoned in Dorchester Prison for six years and released in 1825. He, together with his wife, sister and shopmen, were put into prison in the 1830's, but this did not prevent him from writing numerous political tracts. Hone's prosecution by the Constitutional Association for his scurrilous pamphlet, *Non Mi Ricordo,* concerning the relationship between Queen Caroline and her devoted Italian companion, Bergami, failed, but it helped in the end to imprison a number of radical journalists. Most sensational was the treatment of volunteers who had tried to keep Carlile's magazine *The Republican* going during his own imprisonment. They too were tried, and jailed up for three years in Newgate, where they slept on mats on the stone floor and lived on bread and gruel. 'The astounding circulation figures for the tracts, along with those for the writings of Paine, had enabled the ruling class of England for the first time to grasp in concrete terms the size of the existing public. Every new reader in the lower ranks of society meant another potential victim of radical contagion.[159] After a time the political tract followed in the wake of the religious tract and became so much waste paper to dispose of. Henry Mayhew interviewed a young London pickpocket who said: 'they bring tracts to the lodging-houses — pipes are lighted with them; tracts won't fill your belly. Tracts is no good, except to a person that has a home; and the lodging-houses they're laughed at.'[160]

A. Fletcher's Appeal New influences were at work from the early eighteenth century on which encouraged a breed of passionate, even charismatic, evangelical preachers like William Grimshaw (1703 - 1763), John Wesley and George Whitfield, zealots within the National Church. One of these was the Rev. Alexander Fletcher (1787 - 1860. He came to London from Glasgow in 1811 as Minister of Miles Lane Chapel.. In 1816, he was appointed Minister to the Albion Chapel, and for thirty-five years he was Minister at the Finsbury Circus Chapel, the largest in London. Outwardly he was an upstanding figure in the community, a gifted and Presbyterian divine, whose fame rested principally on his preaching to children, in particular his annual Christmas sermon to the young. Inwardly, he was a man not only of passion, and especially passions. In 1824, Hood did not fail to ignore the scandal that enveloped the universally admired and respected Minister like a whirlwind and whisked him up to a figure of infamy. In a flash, Alexander Fletcher unwillingly joined the canting fraternity to become a butt for the caricaturists and a figure of derision in the print-shops. His involvement with a certain Miss Eliza Dick resulted in a breach of promise action in the civil and ecclesiastical courts. He was summarily suspended by the United Associate Synod of Edinburgh from the exercise of his office and from Church fellowship. In the end, his separation from the secession church was inevitable. Within a few months, the *Trial of the Re. Alexander Fletcher before the United Associate Synod*, was published for all to read. In 1825, Fletcher protested by printing *The Injustice of the United Associate Synod Exposed*. In spite of his disgrace, he was widely supported by his congregation. One of the many caricatures on the topic, published by Marksman of Bishopsgate in 1824[161] shows Fletcher as a slim handsome parson, covering his face with his hands in shame, fleeing from a young woman, and pursued by a flight of arrows representing the press of the day: 'Times', 'Monitor', 'Chronicle', and the clever pun 'Scotch Sin - not' [Synod]. Thomas Hood does not miss a chance to pillory him as one of the canting fraternity:

> Oh, had it pleas'd the gout to take
> The reverend Croly from the stage,
> Or Southey. For our quiet's sake,
> Or Fletcher, Cupid's sage,
> Or damme! namby pamby Poole, —
> or any other clown or fool![17]

Alexander Fletcher gave his last sermon at the Surrey Chapel in February 1860, when nearly 3000 children attended.

Mulock's Let— Thomas Mulock was a minister at Stoke-on-Trent, Staffordshire, where he founded a religious sect. His daughter, Dinah Mary, was known under her married name, Mrs. Craik, the author of *John Halifax, Gentleman.* Halifax wrote against atheism and blasphemy, and published pamphlets and was for a time on the staff of the *Morning Chronicle*. He was born in Dublin and tried at business in Liverpool and failed. He then matriculated at Oxford in 1817 and lectured in Paris in 1820. He was said to have been 'a brilliant, erratic, turbulent Irishman'.[162]

TO BE CONTINUED.

CHRONOLOGY

	Thomas Hood		Contemporary events
		1775	Charles Lamb born
		1786	Burn's Poems. Blake's *Songs of Innocence*
		1788	Byron born
		1789	French Revolution
		1792	Shelley born
		1793	John Clare born
		1795	Keats, Carlyle born
		1796	John Hamilton Reynolds born
		1798	Wordsworth and Coleridge published *Lyrical Ballads*. Pitt introduced income tax
1799	**THOMAS HOOD** born at 3l, The Poultry, in the City of London, on 23rd May		
		1800	Macaulay born
		1801	Jefferson elected President USA
		1804	Napoleon becomes Emperor of France. Disraeli born
		1805	Battle of Trafalgar
		1806	Elizabeth Barrett Browning born
1807	Hood family moved to 5 Lower Street, Islington	1807	Lamb's *Tales from Shakespeare*
		1808	Goethe's *Faust* Part I
		1810	Scott's *Lady of the Lake*
1811	Father and brother died. Family living at Islington.	1811	Thackeray born. Jane Austen's *Sense and Sensibility*.
		1812	Byron's *Childe Harold*
1813	Hood began work in City counting-house		
1814	Probably began to study engraving	1814	Stephenson's *Locomotive*. Napoleon exiled. Restoration of Louis XVIII
1815	Visited Dundee for his health.	1815	Battle of Waterloo.
		1816	Sheridan died. Charlotte Bronte born.
1817	Probably apprenticed as engraver in London	1817	Jane Austen died. Keats *Poems*.
		1818	Keats's *Endymion*. Mary Shelley's *Frankenstein*.

		1820	Accession of George IV
1821	Appointed sub-editor *London Magazine*	1821	Keats died. Scott knighted.
	Friendship with John Hamilton Reynolds		Mill's *Elements of Political Economy*
1822	Became engaged to Jane Reynolds	1822	Shelley died. De Quincey's *Confessions*
		1823	Lamb's *Essays of Elia*
		1824	Byron died. Miss Mitford's *Our Village*
1825	Married Jane Reynolds on 5 May Completed 'Hogarthian' etching *The Progress of Cant.* Collaborated with Reynolds on *Odes and Addresses to Great People.*		
1826	*Whims and Oddities* (Ist Series).	1826	Scott suffers financial ruin.
1827	Thomas and Jane Hood now residing at 2 Robert Street, Adelphi, London. *Whims and Oddities* (2nd Series). *Plea of the Midsummer Fairies* volume. First daughter died as a baby.	1827	Lamb's *On an Infant Dying as Soon Born.* Blake died. Tennyson's first poems.
1828	Severe attack of rheumatic fever.	1828	Webster's *Dictionary.* Catholic Emancipation Act.
1829	Moved to Rose Cottage, Winchmore Hill. Editor *The Gem.* Published *The Dream of Eugene Aram.*		
1830	First *Comic Annual* dedicated to Francis Freeling, Post-Master General. Daughter Frances Freeling born. Began important friendship with Charles Wentworth Dilke.	1830	Hazlitt died. Cobbett's *Rural Rides* Accession of William IV. Charles Wentworth Dilke editor, *The Athenaeum*
1831	*The Dream of Eugene Aram* republished separately. Second *Comic Annual* dedicated to the 6th Duke of Devonshire	1831	Poe's *Poems.* Elliott's *Corn Law Rhymes*
1832	Moved to Lake House, Wanstead, Essex Dedicated third *Comic Annual* to William IV. Audience with the King at the Royal Pavilion, Brighton.	1832	Scott and Crabbe died
		1833	Hartley Coleridge *Poems.* Abolition of slavery in British Colonies.

			Factory Act regulating working conditions.
1834	Novel: *Tylney Hall.* Son Tom born. Serious business failure. Subsequent collapse of finances. Forced into exile.	1834	Death of Lamb and Coleridge. Poor Law Amendment Act.
1835	Hood crossed to Rotterdam in a violent storm. Settled in Coblenz at 372 Castor Hof. Suffered serious ill-health. Friendship with Lieutenant De Franck (19th Polish Regiment).	1835	Cobbett died. Dickens *Boz.* Hans Anderson's *Fairy Tales*
1836	*Ode to Rae Wilson*, Hood's defence of his own liberal views.	1836	Emerson's *Nature*
1837	Moved to 39 Rue Langue, Ostend to be nearer home. Published *Copyright and Copywrong* for the *Athenaeum.*	1837	Dickens *Pickwick Papers.* Carlyle's *French Revolution.* Lamb's *Letters.* Accession of Queen Victoria.
1838	Began work on *Hood's Own*, being a collection of writings largely from the *Comic Annuals.* Suffered further break down in health. Paid brief 'secret' visit to England to consult his doctor.	1838	Dickens *Oliver Twist.* Foundation of Anti-Corn Law League.
1839	*Hood's Own* published.	1839	Dickens *Nicholas Nickelby*
1840	Returned to England permanently. Settled in Camberwell. Began publishing *Miss Kilmansegg and her Precious Leg* in the *New Monthly Magazine.* *Up the Rhine* published. Took legal action against publisher for unfair business dealings. His health deteriorated	1840	Barham's *Ingoldsby Legends.* Poe's *Tales of the Grotesque and Arabesque*
1841	Appointed Editor of *New Monthly Magazine.* Moved to 17 Elm Tree Road, St. John's Wood. Began friendship with Dickens, whose books he reviewed. Supported copyright campaign.	1841	Dickens *Barnaby Rudge* and *The Old Curiosity Shop.* The popular magazine *Punch* started.
1842	Resumed publication of *Comic Annual.*	1842	Macaulay's *Lays.* Tennyson's *Poems.* Wordsworth granted Civil List Pension. Browning's *Dramatic Lyrics.*

				Income tax resumed at 7d in the £ on incomes over £150 per annum (regarded as temporary!)
1843	Moved to Devonshire Lodge, 28 New Finchley Road. *Punch* published *The Song of the Shirt* in its Christmas number and trebled its circulation.		1843	Ruskin's *Modern Painters*. Wordsworth appointed Poet Laureate. Poe's *Murders in the Rue Morgue*.
1844	Began *Hood's Magazine* in spite of serious illness. Published his *Whimsicalities*. Jane Hood granted a Civil List Pension. Hood received a letter of encouragement from Sir Robert Peel.		1844	Elizabeth Barrett Browning's *Poems*. Disraeli's *Coningsby*. Peel's Factory Act.
1845	After a long and protracted illness, **THOMAS HOOD** died on 3rd May, three weeks before his forty-sixth birthday. Buried at Kensal Green Cemetery.		1845	Barham died. Poe's *The Raven*.
			1846	Charlotte, Emily and Anne Bronte's *Poems*. Edward Lear's *Book of Nonsense Verse*.
			1847	Charlotte Bronte's *Jane Eyre*. Emily Bronte's *Wuthering Heights*. Tennyson's *The Princess*.
			1848	Marx and Engel's *Communist Manifesto*. Thackeray's *Vanity Fair*. Tennyson's *In Memoriam*.
			1849	Death of Hartley Coleridge.
			1850	Death of Wordsworth.
			1851	Death of Mary Shelley. Joseph Paxton built Crystal Palace for the Great Exhibition in Hyde Park. First double-decker omnibus. Singer manufactured first practical sewing-machine.
			1852	Matthew Arnold *Poems*. Dickens *Bleak House*.
1854	Stone laid on Hood's 'inscriptionless' grave. The epitaph read: 'He Sang the Song of the Shirt'.		1854	Outbreak of Crimean War. Tennyson's *The Charge of the Light Brigade*

Select Bibliography

1860   Tom Hood and Frances Freeling Broderip: *Collected Works* including *Memorials of Thomas Hood*, (Moxon, Son and Co.)

1869   Tom Hood and Frances Freeling Broderip: *Memorials of Thomas Hood*, revised edition (Moxon, Son and Co.)

1907   Walter Jerrold: *Thomas Hood: His Life and Times* (Alston Rivers)

1911   Walter Jerrold (ed.): *The Complete Poetical Works of Thomas Hood* (Oxford University Press)

1930   Walter Jerrold (ed.): *Thomas Hood and Charles Lamb – The Literary Reminiscences of Thomas Hood* (Ernest Benn Ltd)

1963   J.C. Reid: *Thomas Hood* (Routledge & Kegan Paul)

1968   John Clubbe: *Victorian Forerunner: The Later Career of Thomas Hood* (Duke *University)*

1970   *John* Clubbe: *Selected Poems* (Harvard University)

1972   Lloyd Jeffrey: *Thomas Hood* (Twayne)

1973   Peter F. Morgan: *The Letters of Thomas Hood* (Oliver and Boyd)

1976   Peter Thorogood: *Thomas Hood and 'The Progress of Cant'* (Polytechnic of Central London o.p.)

1981   Peter Thorogood: *Thomas Hood: A Nineteenth Century Author and his Relations with the Book Trade to 1835*
        (Oxford Polytechnic Press ed. Robin Myers and Michael Harris, o.p.)

1982   Joy Flint: *Thomas Hood: Selected Poems* (Carcanet)

1995   Peter Thorogood: *Thomas Hood: Poems Comic and Serious* (Bramber Press)

Notes and References

1. Blackwood's 1843. Included in *Poems* 1844
2. Thomas Hood, *Literary Reminiscences I* – see Walter Jerrold (ed.): *Thomas Hood and Charles Lamb*
3. Walter Jerrold (ed.) *Complete Poetical Works of Thomas Hood*, p411
4. Thomas Hood, *Literary Reminiscences I*
5. *ibid.*
6. *ibid.*
7. Jerrold, *Complete Poetical Works, op. cit.*, p176
8. Thomas Hood, *Literary Reminiscences II*
9. Jerrold, *Complete Poetical Works, op. cit.*, p303
10. Peter F. Morgan, *The Letters of Thomas Hood*, p7, letter to his aunts from Dundee, December 1815
11. c1818. First printed in Alexander Elliott's *Hood in Scotland* pp73-102 (1885)
12. Thomas Hood, *Literary Reminiscences III*
13. *ibid.*
14. Morgan, *op. cit.*, p29, Letter to George Rollo, 11 Oct 1821
15. Jerrold, *Complete Poetical Works, op. cit,* p44
16. Morgan, *op. cit.*, pp25-27, Letter to John Taylor, July 1821
17. Thomas Hood, *Literary Reminiscences V*
18. *ibid.*
19. *ibid.*
20. *ibid.*
21. Bibliog. Gittings, Robert, *The Poetry of John Hamilton Reynolds.* Ariel: Vol. I No.4. October 1970. Jones, Leonidas, Reynolds and Keats. Keats-Shelley journal, Vol VII 1958, pp47-59.
22. Morgan, *op. cit.*, p31, letter to Mrs Charlotte Reynolds, September 1822
23. Morgan, *op. cit.*, p44, letter to Miss Charlotte Reynolds, Nov 1823
24. *Memorials of Thomas Hood*, ed. Frances Broderip and Tom Hood, Moxon, Son & Co. (1869), p43
25. *Memorials, op. cit.*, p30
26. Morgan, *op. cit.*, p65 – Letter to Marianne and Charlotte Reynolds, May 1825
27. Keats: *Endymion* 2 lines 11-19
28. Jerrold, *Complete Poetical Works, op. cit,* II.25-8, p35 Epigraph to Whims and Oddities, 1826
29. George Gilfillan *A Gallery of Literary Portraits* J.M. Dent & co. 1909
30. *Forget-me-not* 1828
31. Blewitt. Jonathan. *The Ballad Singer: A Collection of comical comic songs, selected from 'Whims and Oddities' by T. Hood.* Set to music by J. Blewitt (No.2 'Sally Brown', No.3 'John Trot', No.4 Nelly Gray). 1829. See also *Thomas Hood*, J.C. Reid p117
32. Memorials p32

33. *The Poetical Works of Charles Lamb*. Third Edition. Edward Moxon. London 1838
34. *Memorials* p41
35. *Memorials* p45
36. Quoted in W Jerdan, *The Autobiography of William Jerdan*, London 1852-3, iii, 21
37. *Memorials* p52
38. *Whims and Oddities*. First series. 1826. Jerrold, *Complete Poetical Works, op. cit.*, p44
39. *The Epping Hunt*. Charles Tilt. London. 1829. Jerrold, *Complete Poetical Works, op. cit.*, p197
40. G K Chesterton, *The Victorian Age in Literature* (1913), p18
41. *Memorials* p60
42. Charles MacFarlane (d. 1858), traveller in Italy and Turkey, settled in London and devoted himself to literary work in 1829. Nominated a poor brother of the Charterhouse in 1857. His best works were *Civil and Military History of England*, 8 vols, 1838-44, *The Book of Table Talk*, 1836, and *Reminiscences of a Literary Life*, 1857. Hood never mentions him, which indicates that he was not a close friend and places some doubt on the authenticity of his account of Hood's extravagances.
43. Morgan, *op. cit.*, p225, Letter to Dilke, 17 January 1836, from Coblenz
44. Morgan, *op. cit.*, p209, Letter to John Wright, 31 Dec 1835
45. *Memorials* p70, letter to Jane dated 13 March 1835
46. From *Up the Rhine* - Jerrold, *Complete Poetical Works, op. cit.* p352
47. Morgan, *op. cit.*, p179, Letter to Jane Hood, 19 March 1835
48. *Stanzas on Coming of Age* - Jerrold, *Complete Poetical Works, op. cit.* p244
49. *Memorials* p74 - Letter to Jane Hood, 19 March 1835
50. *Memorials* p76
51. *Memorials* p81
52. Morgan, *op. cit.*, p351, letter to Philip de Franck, December 1837
53. *Memorials* p168 – Letter from Jane Hood to Mrs Elliot, 29 October 1836
54. *Memorials* p169 fn
55. Morgan, *op. cit.*, p453, Letter to Prince Albert, April 1841
56. Morgan, *op. cit.*, p459, letter to Philip de Franck, April 1841
57. *Memorials* p91-2
58. Morgan, *op. cit.*, p244ff, letter to Charles Dilke, 20 June 1836
59. Morgan, *op. cit.*, p260, letter to Charles Wentworth Dilke, 20 June 1836
60. *The Athenaeum*. April 15, 22, and 29, 1837
61. Morgan, *op. cit.*, p298, letter to Philip de Franck, 23 April 1837
62. Morgan, *op. cit.*, p397, letter to Charles Dilke, 7 Nov 1839
63. Morgan, *op. cit.*, 307, letter to John Wright, 30 April 1837
64. Morgan, *op. cit.*, p308, ibid
65. Morgan, *op. cit.*, p316, letter to Dr William Elliot, 26 June 1837
66. *The Athenaeum*, 29 June 1839
67. Morgan, *op. cit.*, p323-4, letter to John Wright, 30 June 1837
68. *Memorials* p238, letter from Hood to Dr Elliot, 2 December 1837

69. *Hoods Own* 1839; Jerrold, *Complete Poetical Works*, *op. cit.*, p274
70. *The Athenaeum* 18321 *Comic Annual 1833*; Jerrold, *Complete Poetical Works*, *op. cit.*, p453 ll. 31-34
71. *Comic Annual* 1834. Jerrold, *Complete Poetical Works*, *op. cit.*, p463
72. *Ode to Rae Wilson.* Athenaeum 1837.
73. Mrs. Carter Hall. *A Book of Memories.* Virtue & Co. London 1871
74. *Memorials* p295-6
75. Baily. 1840
76. *Memorials* p314 – letter to Jane Hood, 15 April 1840
77. *Memorials* p433 – letter from Dr Elliot, 11 May 1840
78. *Memorials* p322 – letter to Jane Hood, April 1840
79. Charles Lamb, *Last Essays of Elia*, published in 1833
80. *Memorials* p 336, letter to De Franck, 13 April 1841
81. *Memorials* p371, letter to Dickens, 12 October 1841
82. *Memorials* p382, letter to De Franck, 14 August 1843
83. *Memorials* p391, letter to Jane from Edinburgh, 27 September 1843
84. Morgan, *op. cit.*, p583, letter to Samuel Phillips, 1 Jan 1844
85. *Punch.* Christmas number.1843; Jerrold, *Complete Poetical Works*, *op. cit.*, p625
86. *Memorials* p406 – letter from Jane Hood to Dr Elliot, 22 May 1844
87. *Hood's Magazine* May 1844
88. *Hood's Magazine* May 1844; Jerrold, *Complete Poetical Works*, *op. cit.* p649.
89. *Memorials* p420
90. *Memorials* p423, letter to Phillips, September 1844
91. *Memorials* p427
92. *Hood's Magazine* November 1844; Jerrold, *Complete Poetical Works*, *op. cit.*, p651
93. *Hood's Magazine* February 1844, Jerrold, *Complete Poetical Works*, *op. cit.*, p641
94. *Memorials* p436 – letter to Robert Peel, 10 November 1844
95. *Memorials* p 439 – letter to Dr Elliot, 17 November 1844
96. *Memorials* p458
97. *Memorials* p461fn
98. Morgan, *op. cit.*, p446, letter to Thomas Noon Talfourd, January 1841
99. John Murray, ed., *Lord Byron's Correspondence* (1922), II, 90. Letter to John Cam Hobhouse, 11 November 1818
100. *The Idler*. 29 September 1759
101. Laurence Sterne, *Tristram Shandy* (1760-67) III.12
102. M. Dorothy George, *Catalogue of Political and Personal Satires.* Department of Prints and Drawings, British Museum. X, no.13764
103. Graham Hewitt, *English Caricaturists and Graphic Humorists of the Nineteenth Century.* (1893) pp. 80-81 and plate facing p81
104. Thomas Love Peacock, *Crotchet Castle.* (1831) ch.7
105. W. H. Merle, *Odds and Ends* (1853) Quoted by M. Dorothy George, *op. cit.* X, xi
106. Peacock, *op. cit.* ch.7

107.E.L. McAdam, Jr. and George Milne, eds. *Johnson's Dictionary: a Modern Selection* (1963) p.113

108.*Westminster Review*, June 1840

109.Charles Dickens, *Pickwick Papers* (1836 -37) ch.30

110.M. Dorothy George, *op. cit.* X, 472 - 473, no. 14773

111.Charles Knight, *Passages from a Working Life* (1864) I.259

112.Morgan, *op. cit.*, p.66,   Letter to Mrs. Charlotte Reynolds, 9 November 1825

113.*New Monthly Magazine*, XVI (February 1826), 232

114.*London Magazine*, IV (January 1826), 45 – 46

115.William Hone, *Everyday Book* (1827) II.131

116.M. Dorothy George*, op. cit.* X, xxxiii

117.*vide* British Weekly, 8 October 1936

118.M. Dorothy George, *op. cit.* X, No. 13762

119.Charles Dickens, *Bleak House* (1852 - 53) ch.4

120.*Ibid.*, ch.8

121.Joseph Haydn, *Dictionary of dates and Universal Information* (1841) p. 797

122.M. Dorothy George, *op. cit.* X, xxiii

123.*Dictionary of National Biography* 1911 ed. X, 294-295

124.British Museum BM 14812

125.*London Magazine*, IV (January 1826) 45

126.British Museum BM 14812

127.M. Dorothy George*, English Political Caricature* 1783 - 1832 (1959) p. 204

128.M. Dorothy George, *Catalogue of Political and Personal Satires*, X, 181n

129.Peacock, *op. cit.,* ch.2

130.Thomas Moore, *Tom Cribb's Memorial, by One of the Fancy* (1819)

131.Arthur Rubens, in *Transactions of the Jewish Historical Society* XXIII, 97

132.*Gentleman's Magazine* (July 1822) pp. 9-11

133.British Museum B.M.L. 1875 7/8

134.Hone, *op. cit.*, col.133

135.Allardyce Nicoll, *Early Nineteenth Century Drama*, I, 18

136.*Eclectic Review*, XIX (March 1846), 288.   See also John Clubbe, *Victorian Forerunner: the Later Career of Thomas Hood* (1968) pp. 17 and 202n

137.*Dictionary of National Biography*   XLI 377

138.Hone, *op. cit.*, cols. 129-131

139.Shakespeare, *Hamlet*, XXX, i

140."Ode to William Kitchener MD" in *Odes and Addresses* (1825)

141.Charles Baudelaire, *Art in Paris*, 1845 - 62.   Translated and edited by Jonathan Mayne (1965)

142.V. S. Pritchett, *The Living Novel* (1954) p.60

143.William Makepeace Thackeray, Congreve and Addison, in *English Humorists* (1853)

144.Shakespeare, *Hamlet*, III, i

145.Richard Altick, *English Common Reader: A Social History of the Mass Reading Public*, 1800-1900

146.*Complete Poetical Works of Thomas Hood*, p31, v8

147.Hone, *op. cit.*, Col 134

148.*Complete Poetical Works*, p563 ll. 145 - 148

149.*New Sporting Magazine* 1832

150.M. Dorothy George, *op. cit.*, Vol X pp495-6

151.M. Dorothy George, *op. cit.*, Vol X pp443-4

152.Isaac Watts, *Against Lying*

153.*Complete Poetical Works*, p18

154.*New Monthly Magazine*, XVI (February 1826), 232.

155.Everitt, *op. cit.*, p101

156.M. Dorothy George, *op. cit.*, Vol X 450 -1 No 14711 cf. 13975

157.G.H. Spinney, *Cheap Repository Tracts*. See Library Ser. 4. XX (1939) pp. 295 - 304

158.Richard Altick, *op. cit.*, p70

159.Altick, *op. cit.*, p76

160.*London Labour and the London Poor* 1861

161.M Dorothy George, *op. cit.*, Vol XXX p442 No 14700

162.John S. Crone *Dictionary of Irish Biography*, Longmans Green, 1928

INDEX

9 781905 206179